AN AGE OF SCIENCE AND REVOLUTIONS, 1600–1800

THE MEDIEVAL & EARLY MODERN WORLD

BONNIE G. SMITH

GENERAL EDITOR

AN AGE OF SCIENCE AND REVOLUTIONS, 1600–1800

Toby E. Huff

OXFORD
UNIVERSITY PRESS

*To the memory of Dr. Shaukat Ali (1923–2003), a dear colleague of three decades,
and to my indispensable support system: Judith, Erik, and Niki*

OXFORD
UNIVERSITY PRESS

Oxford University Press, Inc., publishes works that further
Oxford University's objective of excellence
in research, scholarship, and education.

Oxford New York
Auckland Cape Town Dar es Salaam Hong Kong Karachi
Kuala Lumpur Madrid Melbourne Mexico City Nairobi
New Delhi Shanghai Taipei Toronto

With offices in
Argentina Austria Brazil Chile Czech Republic France Greece
Guatemala Hungary Italy Japan Poland Portugal Singapore
South Korea Switzerland Thailand Turkey Ukraine Vietnam

Copyright © 2005 by Oxford University Press, Inc.

Published by Oxford University Press, Inc.
198 Madison Avenue, New York, New York 10016
www.oup.com

Oxford is a registered trademark of Oxford University Press

Design: Stephanie Blumenthal and Alexis Siroc
Cover design and logo: Nora Wertz
Layout: Alexis Siroc

Library of Congress Cataloging-in-Publication Data

Huff, Toby E., 1942–
An age of science and revolutions, 1600-1800 / Toby Huff.
p. cm. — (Medieval & early modern world)
ISBN-13: 978-019-517724-4 — 978-019-522157-2 (set) — 978-019-522269-2 (Calif. ed.)
ISBN-10: 0-19-517724-X — 0-19-522157-5 (set) — 0-19-522269-5 (Calif. ed.)
1. History, Modern—17th century—Juvenile literature. 2. History, Modern—18th century--Juvenile literature.
3. Europe—Civilization--17th century—Juvenile literature. 4. Europe—Civilization—18th century—
Juvenile literature. I. Title. II. Medieval and early modern world.
D246.H83 2005
909'.6--dc22
2004021612

9 8 7 6 5 4 3 2 1

Printed in the United States on acid-free paper.

On the cover: An 18th-century armillary sphere (center), used to determine the positions of
heavenly bodies; a manuscript page from Voltaire's *Candide, or Optimism* (1759).
Frontispiece: An early 17th-century painting entitled *The Arts and Sciences.*

BONNIE G. SMITH

GENERAL EDITOR

DIANE L. BROOKS, Ed. D.

EDUCATION CONSULTANT

CONTENTS

A 66 marks a primary source—a piece of writing or an artifact that speaks to us from the past.

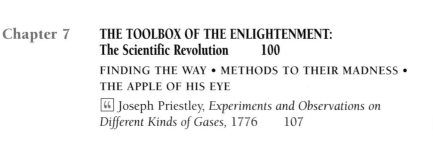

CAST OF CHARACTERS

Akbar (AHK-bahr) **the Great,** 1542–1605 • Effective Mughal ruler who promoted religious toleration

Aurangzeb (oh-rahng-ZEHB), 1618–1707 • Mughal ruler involved in a war of succession with his brothers

Babur (BAH-buhr), 1483–1530 • Founder of the Mughal Empire

Bacon, Francis, 1561–1626 • Englishman who championed the scientific method and encouraged use of experiments

Bobovi (boh-BOH-vee), **Albert** (Ali Bey), 17th century • Polish page who lived and worked in the Ottoman sultan's palace in the 1630s

Brahe (BRAH-hay), **Tycho** (TEE-ko), 1546–1601 • Danish astronomer who made many accurate observations and discovered the first supernova

Charles I, 1600–1649 • English king executed in 1649 after losing a power struggle with Parliament that sparked the English Civil War

Confucius (con-FYU-shus), 551–479 BCE • Influential Chinese philosopher who emphasized respect for parents and other basic values

Copernicus (kuh-PER-nih-kuhs), **Nicolaus,** 1473–1543 • Polish mathematician who developed sun-centered theory of the universe

Cromwell, Oliver, 1599–1658 • British general who assumed the title of Lord Protector in 1653 after overthrowing Charles I in the English Civil War

Descartes (day-CART), **René** (ruh-NAY), 1596–1650 • Mathematician and philosopher who proclaimed, "I think, therefore I am"

Diderot (DEE-der-o), **Dénis** (day-NEESS), 1713–1784 • Philosopher who organized and edited the French *Encyclopédie*

Elizabeth I, 1533–1603 • Queen of England during its defeat of the Spanish Armada

Equiano (eh-kwee-AHN-o), **Olaudah** (oh-LAU-dah), around 1744–1797 • African writer and former slave whose 1789 autobiography shed light on the cruelty and injustice of the slave trade, including the infamous "middle passage"

Falconbridge, Alexander, died 1792 • British surgeon who traveled on slave ships during the 18th century and later wrote about the appalling conditions aboard these ships

Franklin, Benjamin, 1706–1790 • American writer, scientist, and statesman

Galilei (gah-luh-LAY), **Galileo** (gah-luh-LAY-o), 1564–1642 • Italian astronomer and mathematician who used the telescope to discover the craters of the moon

Geoffrin (joff-RIHN), **Marie Thérèse** (mah-REE tay-REHZ), 1699–1777 • Hostess of a salon that supported the writing of the *Encyclopédie*

Gosnold, Bartholomew, 1577–1607 • English explorer who discovered the coast of Maine in 1602 and gave Cape Cod its name

Grotius (GROH-shee-us), **Hugo,** 1583–1645 • Dutchman who believed rational inquiry could uncover a "natural law" for universal standards of human conduct

Harvey, William 1578–1657 • English physician who studied the circulatory system of the body

al-Haytham (ahl-hah-EE-thum), **ibn** (IH-bin), 956–1040 • Egyptian mathematician and pioneer in optics

Herschel (HER-shul), **Caroline,** 1750–1848 • German-born astronomer who was the first woman to discover a comet

Herschel (HER-shul), **Sir William,** 1738–1822 • German-born astronomer renowned for discovering the planet Uranus in 1781, among other astronomical accomplishments

Hutchinson, Thomas, 1711–1780 • American governor of colonial Massachusetts who was the symbol of loyalty to Britain in pre-Revolutionary Boston

Jahangir (juh-HAHN-geer), 1569–1627 • Mughal ruler, son of Akbar the Great

Jai Sing (jai SING), 1686–1743 • Indian governor, mathematician, astronomer, and city planner

James II, 1633–1701 • English king who abdicated his claim to the throne

John, 1167–1216 • An unjust English king who was forced by barons to sign the great constitutional document the Magna Carta (Great Charter) in 1215

Kepler (KEH-pler), **Johannes** (YO-hahn-ess), 1571–1630 • German mathematician and astronomer who discovered the laws of planetary motion, proving Nicolaus Copernicus's heliocentric theory

Kochu Bey (ko-CHOO BAY) died 1650 • Albanian or Macedonian scholar, recruited as a young boy to serve in the Ottoman Empire, who became Grand Vizier

Lambert (lahm-BARE), **Anne Thérèse de** (tay-REHZ duh), 1647–1733 • French marquess famous for hosting biweekly meetings of scholars, writers, and artists in her salon

Lippershey (LIH-per-shee), **Hans** (HAHNS), around 1570–1619 • Dutch lensmaker credited with creating the first practical telescope in 1608

Locke, John, 1632–1704 • English philosopher who championed constitutional government

Lufti Pasha (loof-TEE pah-SHA), 1488–1563 • Albanian or Macedonian scholar recruited as a young boy to serve in the Ottoman Empire, who became Grand Vizier in the mid-16th century

Mahal (mah-HAHL), **Mumtaz** (muhm-TAHZ), 1593–1631 • Niece of Nur Jahan and wife of Shah Jahan. Her death in childbirth inspired her grieving husband to build the Taj Mahal as a tribute to her memory

Malpighi (mahl-PEE-gee), **Marcello** (mahr-CHEHL-o), 1628–1694 • Italian physician who discovered the capillaries connecting the arteries and the veins in the human body

Mary II, 1662–1694 • English queen. The daughter of James II and Anne Hyde, she was married to William III

Mercator (mer-KAY-ter), **Gerhardus** (jehr-AHR-duhs), 1512–1594 • Born Gerhard Kremer, Flemish mapmaker who invented the Mercator projection, a more accurate and practical method of portraying the round earth on a flat map

Montagu (MON-tah-gyew), **Mary Wortley** (WERT-lee), **Lady,** 1689–1762 • Introduced to England the method of inoculating against smallpox, which she learned in Turkey

Montesquieu (mon-teh-SKYUH), **Baron de** (bah-RON duh), 1689–1755 • Philosopher and writer who proposed the separation of the powers of government

More, Hannah, 1745–1833 • English feminist, writer, and philanthropist

Mundy, Peter, 1608–1667 • English traveler and East India Company official who wrote about India

Muteferrika (MOO-tuh-FER-ih-kuh), **Ibrahim** (ee-brah-HEEM), 1674–1742 • Hungarian convert to Islam who operated the first officially accepted printing press in the Ottoman Empire

Newton, Isaac, Sir, 1642–1727 • English scientist who defined the three laws of motion, including the law of gravity

Nur Jahan (NOOR juh-HAHN), 1577–1645 • Wife of Sultan Jahangir and Empress of India who commissioned the building of great monuments

Philip II, 1527–1598 • Spanish Catholic king who launched the Armada and fought against Protestant reformers

Polo, Marco, 1253?–1324 • Venetian adventurer who spent many years traveling through China

Priestley, Joseph, 1733–1804 • English scientist and clergyman who helped to discover oxygen

Ptolemy (TAH-luh-mee), 2nd century CE • Greek astronomer who lived and studied in Alexandria, Egypt

Ricci (REE-chee), **Matteo** (mah-TAY-o), 1552–1610 • Jesuit missionary who traveled to China to convert people to Christianity and introduced them to Western scientific instruments and concepts

Rousseau (roo-SO), **Jean-Jacques** (zhahn-ZHAHK), 1712–1788 • French author, philosopher, and political theorist who wrote *The Social Contract*

Shah Jahan (SHAH juh-HAHN) 1592–1666 • Ruler of Mughal India who built the Taj Mahal in memory of his wife, Mumtaz Mahal

Sinan (see-NAHN), 1489–1588 • Renowned Ottoman architect who rebuilt Istanbul for Suleiman I

Smith, Adam, 1723–1790 • Economist known as the "father of modern economics," wrote the influential work *The Wealth of Nations.*

Suleiman I (soo-lay-MAHN), 1494–1566 • Ottoman ruler known as "Suleiman the Magnificent"

Ulloa (oo-LYO-uh), **Antonio De** (ahn-TOH-nee-o duh), 1714–1795 • Spanish naval officer who traveled to Peru in 1735 on a scientific expedition and recorded his observations about the lives of native Peruvians

Ulug Beg (oo-LOOG BEHG), 1394–1449 • Turkish mathematician and astronomer who built an observatory in Sarmakand, Uzbekistan

Voltaire (vohl-TAIR), 1694–1778 • Born François-Marie Arouet, philosopher, novelist, political essayist

Washington, George, 1732–1799 • American general and statesman, first president of the United States

Wesley, John, 1703–1791 • Founder of Methodism

William III, 1650–1702 • English king, accepted the Declaration of Rights establishing major principles of constitutional government

Wollstonecraft (WUHL-stehn-craft), **Mary,** 1759–1797 • Feminist author, wrote *Vindication of the Rights of Women*

Zhu Xi (joo shee), 1130–1200 • Neo-Confucian philosopher who developed a system of instruction

Zhu Yizhun (joo ee-jwun), 1573–1620 • Chinese emperor who ruled for 48 years, neglecting his duties

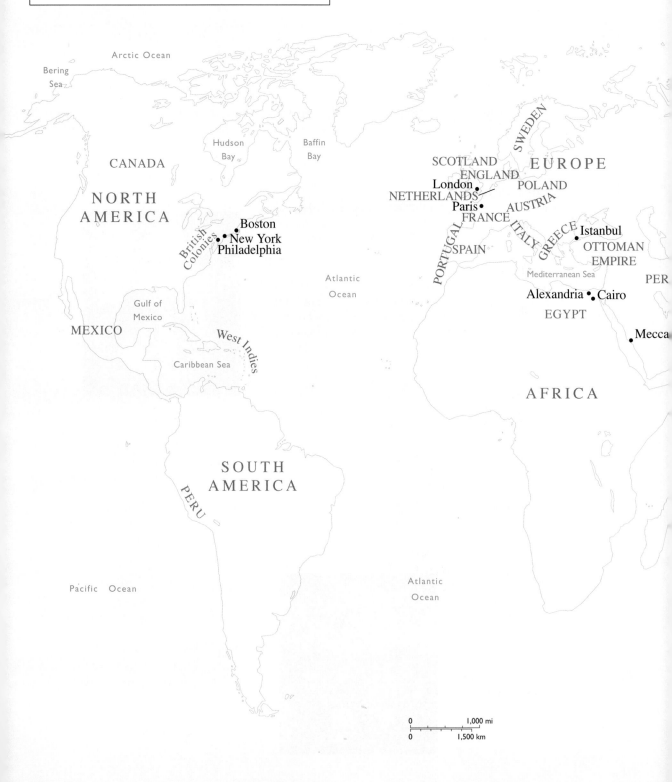

THE WORLD OF SCIENCE AND REVOLUTIONS, 1600—1800

Arctic Ocean

Bering
Sea

CANADA

NORTH
AMERICA

Hudson
Bay

Baffin
Bay

British
Colonies

Boston
New York
Philadelphia

Atlantic
Ocean

Gulf of
Mexico

MEXICO

West Indies

Caribbean Sea

SOUTH
AMERICA

PERU

Pacific Ocean

Atlantic
Ocean

SCOTLAND
ENGLAND
London
NETHERLANDS
Paris
FRANCE

SWEDEN

EUROPE

POLAND

AUSTRIA

ITALY

PORTUGAL

SPAIN

GREECE

Istanbul

OTTOMAN
EMPIRE

Mediterranean Sea

PER

Alexandria Cairo

EGYPT

Mecca

AFRICA

0 ———— 1,000 mi
0 ———— 1,500 km

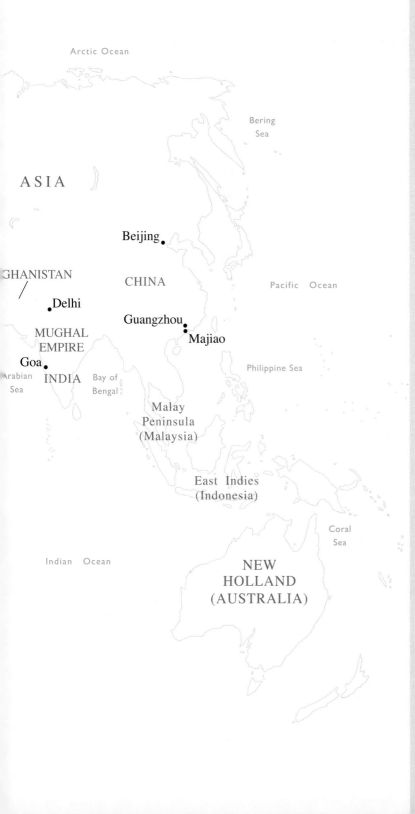

Arctic Ocean

Bering
Sea

ASIA

Beijing

GHANISTAN

CHINA

Pacific Ocean

Delhi

Guangzhou

MUGHAL
EMPIRE

Majiao

Goa

Arabian
Sea

INDIA

Bay of
Bengal

Philippine Sea

Malay
Peninsula
(Malaysia)

East Indies
(Indonesia)

Coral
Sea

Indian Ocean

NEW
HOLLAND
(AUSTRALIA)

SOME PRONUNCIATIONS

Beijing (bay-jing)

Cairo (KY-ro)

Constantinople (kahn-STAN-tehn-OH-puhl)

Delhi (DEH-lee)

Goa (GO-uh)

Guangzhou (gwahng-jo)

Istanbul (IS-tehn-buhl)

Majiao (mah-jeeaow)

Malay (muh-LAY)

Mughal (MOO-guhl)

INTRODUCTION
WHAT IS ENLIGHTENMENT?

In 1784, the philosopher Immanuel Kant wrote an essay entitled "What Is Enlightenment?" In the essay, he answered his own question: "Enlightenment is man's release from his self-incurred tutelage." He went on to explain that tutelage was a person's inability to think for himself. For many centuries before Kant's time, people had king and clergy to tell them what to think and how to think it. The tutelage was self-imposed, Kant claimed, not because people *cannot* think for themselves, but because it takes courage and resolution to do so. His motto for the Enlightenment was "Dare to know!"

During the Enlightenment, a time of intellectual awakening in the 18th century, courageous men and women broke with tradition, often under threat of exile, imprisonment, or even death, in order to share their new understanding of the world around them—an understanding different from what they had been taught by both church and state. For Europeans at that time, the Bible was their science and their morality; it regulated their holidays and many aspects of daily life. This new way of thinking gave them a scientific approach not only to nature, but to political and social issues as well.

Kant realized that this awakening was only a beginning. "If we are asked, 'Do we now live in an enlightened age?' the answer is, 'No,' but we do live in an age of enlightenment." He compared this new act of free thinking to a seed—a seed just emerging from its hard shell. But as the seed took root in society, Kant saw how the Enlightenment moved people from unthinking to freethinking. It "gradually works back upon the character of the people, who thereby gradually become capable of managing freedom; finally, it affects the principles of government, which finds it to its advantage to treat men, who are now more than machines, in accordance with their dignity."

The years between 1600 and 1800 were among the most innovative and exciting in the history of the world. It was the era of the Scientific Revolution as well as the Enlightenment. These two intellectual movements were charged by the belief in the power of human reason. Intellectual leaders during this time believed that their intelligence gave humans the power to understand the patterns of nature without the guidance of religion. For example, astronomers studying the heavens concluded, contrary to the teachings of Christianity, that the earth was not the center of the universe. Other scientists worked out with mathematical precision the exact motions of the planets and stars in the sky. Still others explored the structure of the human body. These intellectual achievements convinced many Europeans that the powers of human reason, however flawed and mistaken they could be, were capable of understanding and explaining the secrets of nature.

This confidence in reasoned inquiry then spread to the moral and political world. European philosophers, lawyers, and others began to ask questions about social customs and political traditions that put kings and nobles ahead of ordinary people. They wanted to know what arrangements were best suited to promoting human happiness. Explorations around the globe during this time made Europeans aware of different social customs and political systems that existed in faraway cultures. Reports by men and women from England, France, the Netherlands, and other countries on these customs and political systems flooded from the new printing presses that were adopted across Europe in the 16th and 17th centuries. Reading these reports provoked a great deal of debate and discussion. Europeans wanted to know the differences between their customs and those of China, India, and the Middle East. They wanted to know how people could justify following

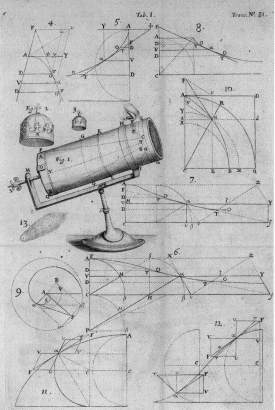

Isaac Newton's sketch of the telescope he designed shows a concave, or inward-curving, lens and a flat mirror to direct light to the viewer. Newton's studies helped establish the new, mathematically precise description of our universe that is at the center of modern astronomy.

Chapitre XXIV

This handwritten and edited page is from a draft of Voltaire's novel Candide, or Optimism. Published in 1759, the novel is filled with humorous criticisms of French society, including its religious leaders. As a result of his bold writings, Voltaire spent much of his life living in exile.

one set of customs as opposed to another. They also asked whether kings had a divine right to rule and how human rights could be made to prevail in the face of oppressive rulers.

Out of such debates came political action. Europeans and Americans undertook major changes in their political systems in order to improve government and preserve human rights. It was out of such debates and action that the idea of constitutional government was established. This was the idea that governments ought to be shaped and controlled by agreed-upon rules and procedures. It also included the idea that one set of government officials should oversee the actions and decisions of others. This meant that rulers could not make all the laws by themselves. This sharing of power would create a system of "checks and balances."

Another key part of this new system of governance was the idea that the people should participate. The idea emerged that political officials should be elected by the people—the implication being that kings and other rulers did not have a divine right to govern. They needed the consent of the people.

While these political and social changes were taking shape in Europe, important new contacts were being established between Europeans and the rest of the world. Europeans in the 17th century continued their efforts to explore and then colonize distant parts of the world. This was especially true of North America. Spanish, English, Dutch, and French adventurers explored the Atlantic coast of North America and then began to establish settlements among the Native Americans.

During this same period, other Europeans set sail for India and China, hoping to find treasures of spices, silver, and gold. The populations of India and China, however, were more resistant to the Europeans than were the Native Americans. But nevertheless, Europeans were able to develop strong commercial ties with Indian and Chinese merchants.

In the Middle East, around the Mediterranean Sea, Europeans faced the military and naval presence of the Ottomans. Unlike the Native Americans, who were overwhelmed by European colonists, these Muslim rulers kept the Europeans on the defensive, launching military campaigns into the eastern European countries. By the 1650s, the Ottoman Turks ruled almost the entire southern Mediterranean coast, from the city of Algiers on the coast of Algeria, all the way into eastern Europe (what is now Romania, Albania, Bosnia-Hercegovina and Serbia, and parts of Croatia and Hungary). They held territories along the Adriatic Sea all the way into Hungary. In 1683 the Turks launched their last and unsuccessful assault on the gates of Vienna. In the meantime, Europeans tried to defeat the Ottomans both by land and by sea—the French attacked

Men gather in a public coffeehouse in Istanbul to discuss politics, catch up on the day's news, and, of course, drink coffee. These coffeehouses were just one feature of Ottoman culture that impressed visiting Europeans, who were hungry for knowledge of how others lived. The Europeans brought such ideas back to their own cities.

Algeria, for example, in an attempt to stop Ottoman piracy. Nevertheless, trade relations between Europeans and the Ottomans increased.

Despite resistance to European influences in places like India and China, zealous missionaries from Europe attempted to win new converts to Christianity. This was especially true of the followers of the Society of Jesus, or Jesuits. They sent dozens of missionaries off to India and to China.

Although the Jesuit missionaries did not largely succeed in converting new Christians, they did bring back to Europe a rich cargo of knowledge about other peoples, along with commercial goods. Indeed, by learning Chinese and creating a Chinese-Latin dictionary, some of the Jesuits laid the foundations for scholarly study of Chinese civilization. At the same time, they helped to spread throughout the world knowledge from the Far East as well as the many new scientific ideas that were then emerging in Europe.

The Scientific Revolution and the Enlightenment created many new scientific ideas and new concepts about the ideal forms of government. The Enlightenment also helped to create a new appreciation of the diversity of other peoples around the globe. The belief that scientific study will continue to bring powerful insights into the structure of the natural world is a major legacy of this Age of Enlightenment. Likewise, the idea of representative government based on the consent of the people and a "bill of rights" came from this exciting period. It was an era that saw greater participation of people in the government, and an era in which women began to play a greater role in intellectual and scientific life. Kant's motto represents the spirit of the times: "Dare to know!"

CHAPTER 1

SETTLEMENTS, TRADE, AND CONFLICT

THE NORTH AMERICAN EXPERIENCE

By the time Bartholomew Gosnold, a sea captain from Suffolk, England, began exploring the coast of New England in 1602, the Spanish had already established many settlements in the New World. Spanish conquistadors, or conquerors, had looted their way from Florida west to Mexico, down the Central American peninsula, and into South America. Everywhere the Spanish went, they grabbed treasure in exchange for disease and death. Their treasure was in the obvious form—gold and silver—but also took the form of new foods such as potatoes and corn. (At first, however, Europeans did not consider potatoes treasures at all—they thought that the lumpy, pocked root transmitted leprosy.)

Toward the end of Queen Elizabeth I's reign, Gosnold and other Englishmen were looking for new opportunities for trade. They also hoped to find a "northwest passage" around (or through) the new American continent that many saw as nothing more than a giant roadblock between them and India.

In 1602, Gosnold and 32 others set sail on the *Concord*. The 30-ton ship carried 8 sailors, 12 passengers planning to return to England, and another 12 travelers who were planning to stay at the trading post Gosnold hoped to set up once he reached the New World.

Toward the end of their voyage, when the crew began to spot

Captain Bartholomew Gosnold (center, in large hat) trades knives and other items with Native Americans on the Virginia shore. Years after his first explorations of the coast of Maine and Cape Cod, Gosnold returned to America as one of the first settlers at Jamestown. Relations between the natives and settlers were often strained, but they carried on a valuable trade together.

signs of land—birds overhead and floating weeds brushing the hull—the leadsman took his post on deck. He cast out a long line with a lead weight tied to the end. Colorful cloth knots placed at intervals that spanned the distance of his two outstretched arms marked each fathom on the line. Shouting out the depths to the ocean's bottom to his helper, he recorded future fishing banks as the ship neared the rocky coast of what was later named Maine, but which the crew called Northland.

It wasn't long before Gosnold and his men met their first Native Americans near a place he called Savage Rock. The English had never kept records during a voyage to the New World before, so imagine their shock when the natives of this new world sailed up in a European-style boat rigged with sails just like their own. They were even more surprised to see some of the natives dressed in European clothing and to hear them speak "Christian" words. In his ship's log, Gosnold wrote, "A Biscay shallop [small ship] with mast, sail, iron grapnel and a copper kettle, with eight native sailors....clothed more or less in European costume, came boldly on shipboard...with a piece of chalk they mapped out the new country."

Following the chalk map the Native Americans had drawn for them, Gosnold and his crew sailed southward along the coast on a steady breeze until they entered a bay protected by an enormous arm of land. It took a day to figure out how the cape connected to the mainland, and while they were exploring, the crew fished. They caught so many cod on that hot and humid spring afternoon that there was

"[T]o give their character in a worde, they are as proper men and women for feature and limbes as can be founde, for flesh and bloud as active."

—New England colonist Thomas Morton, on the Indians, *New English Canaan*, 1637

no room on the ship for the whole catch, and the men had to toss many fish back into the bay. After Gosnold and his crew feasted on fresh cod for dinner, Gosnold wrote in his log the new name for this cape—Cape Cod.

When it was time to leave Cape Cod Bay, a crewman named Tucker climbed to the crow's nest for lookout duty. What he saw scared him so much he must have screamed with terror to the captain below. White water—everywhere! Shoals! The ship was doomed to run aground. They would all die. A square-rigged ship such as the *Concord* is hard to maneuver because it is hard to turn the sails to the wind, but somehow the ship's master and the *very* determined crew steered her clear of the shallows and out of Cape Cod Bay. When the *Concord* reached the seaward side of Cape Cod, once again safely in deep waters, Gosnold told his crew those shoals were to be known forever as "Tucker's Terror."

Gosnold was one of the first English commercial adventurers to explore and try to settle along the northeast coast of America. But Gosnold wasn't quite ready to settle in yet. He and his passengers looked for ways to make a profit. In the past, Gosnold had made at least one piracy run, filling his ship with booty, but now he was looking for a safer way to earn money. So he and his passengers and crew set out in search of sassafras (a substance made from tree bark), cedar, and gold. Today sassafras is used to flavor root beer, but at that time Europeans considered it a cure-all. They believed it could cure toothaches, stomachaches, joint pain, infertility, and just about anything else that ailed them. On an island off Cape Cod the sailors found sassafras trees and collected their bark, working hard to fill their ship with this profitable "wonder drug."

When the *Concord* was loaded with cedar and sassafras, the 12 passengers who originally intended to stay and build a settlement took a good look at

LAURUS Sassafras.

Sassafras, probably named by the Spanish, is a plant native to eastern North America that was avidly sought by European explorers of the 16th and 17th centuries. It was so popular as a cure-all in Europe that it became a major reason for journeying to the New World.

the food supply and realized they would never make it through the winter. At stops along the coast, they had heard the stories of the hardships colonists faced in the first few years, and just how difficult it had been for them to survive. They knew that many colonists had starved. And so they all sailed back to England. Once they were on open seas, the captain ordered the crew to cut loose the shallop to make better time. Is this an order captains often gave? If so, it might explain how the Native Americans at Savage Rock came by their Biscay shallop.

The *Concord* made it home in just 35 days. It would be more than three years before Gosnold returned to America. When he did, in 1606, he served as second-in-command on

In 1622, the London businessmen who promoted the Virginia colony published a list of recommended supplies that potential colonists should bring with them when they settled there. The hardships of Virginia's early settlers were well known, and this damaged the colony's ability to attract new settlers. The list helped ensure that colonists would feel more confident about settling in Virginia.

THE INCONVENIENCIES THAT HAVE HAPPENED TO SOME PERSONS WHICH HAVE TRANSPORTED THEMSELVES from *England* to *Virginia*, without provisions necessary to sustaine themselues, hath greatly hindred the Progresse of that noble Plantation: For preuention of the like disorders heereafter, that no man suffer, either through ignorance or misinformation; it is thought requisite to publish this short declaration: wherein is contained a particular of such necessaries, as either priuate families or single persons shall haue cause to furnish themselues with, for their better support at their first landing in Virginia; whereby also greater numbers may receiue in part, directions how to prouide themselues.

Imprinted at London by FELIX KYNGSTON. 1622.

"[S]uch Majestie…which oftentimes strykes awe and sufficient wonder in our people"

—Englishman William Strachey on Chief Powhatan, *Historie of Travell*, 1612

a ship named the *Godspeed.* This time Gosnold would not go back to England with his passengers. In fact, Gosnold would never see his home again. The 108 passengers on the *Godspeed* were determined to set up the first successful English colony on the east coast of America. They knew that New World explorers faced hazardous living conditions. Even in the warmer southern regions water supplies could be contaminated, food supplies short, and diseases ever-present. Without experience in the new land, settlers found it difficult to grow enough food for a whole colony. The European colonists depended almost totally on Native Americans. Here, Native Americans, not Europeans, were masters of the land.

After three weeks of sailing up and down the James River, the colonists on the *Godspeed* chose a small pear-shaped peninsula on which to build their new settlement. They called it Jamestown in honor of the new English monarch, King James. The peninsula was located about 150 miles south of today's Washington, D.C.

Gosnold didn't like the location at all. The land was swampy and infested with mosquitoes that carried malaria, a disease characterized by high fever and chills. When the tide came in, seawater covered half the peninsula. And it was smack in the middle of Native American territory. But deep water along the bank allowed ships to come in close for loading and unloading, so the *Godspeed*'s passengers overruled Gosnold. It turned out Gosnold was right to be concerned about the conditions at Jamestown. That first summer, 50 of the colonists died, Gosnold among them. By the time the first supply ship arrived in 1608, only 38 of the original 108 settlers were left.

"One of the chiefest standing before them crosse-legged, with his Arrow readie in his Bow in one hand, and taking a Pipe of Tobacco in the other, with a bold uttering of his speech, demanded of us our being there, willing us to bee gone. Wee made signes of peace, which they perceived in the end, and let us land in quietnesse."

—Jamestown settler George Percy, *Observations by Master George Percy,* 1607

In 1612, Captain John Smith published a book that described the land, people, and government of Virginia and included a detailed map of the colony. Powhatan, the Native American chief who persuaded the colonists to live in cooperation with the natives, is the central figure in the illustration in the map's upper left-hand corner.

Captain John Smith, who led the settlement, had been captured in 1607 by the local American Indians after they ambushed him and his companions. This branch of the Iroquois that the English called the Powhatans held Smith captive for about four weeks before releasing him unharmed. The Native American leader whom Captain Smith named Powhatan pointed out the advantages to both sides of peaceful cooperation. It was better than the use of violence and force. According to Smith, the chief asked the Englishmen, "What will it availe you to take that by force you may quickly have by love, or to destroy them that provide you food. What can you get by warre, when we can hide our provisions and fly to the woods? whereby you must famish by wronging us your friends." Powhatan cautioned the Englishmen not to underestimate the Indians, saying, "Think you I am so simple, not to know it is better to eate good meate, lye well, and sleepe quietly with my women and children, laugh and be merry with you, have copper, hatchets, or what I want being your friend: then be forced to flie from all, to lie cold in the woods, . . . and be so hunted by you, that I can neither rest, eate, nor sleepe."

The message was clear: The natives could hide and keep their food supply to themselves, and the colonists would starve to death, or they could cooperate. Over the course of native-white relations, sometimes the whites took Powhatan's advice; but sometimes they didn't, and the result was bloodshed.

RISKY BUSINESS

Although some of the Jamestown settlers died from disease, those losses were an insignificant blip compared to the numbers of Native Americans who suffered a similar fate. One of the tragic results of the intermingling of peoples from across the globe with North and South Americans was the spread of disease—and with it, a vast destruction of Native American peoples. Illnesses such as malaria, yellow fever, influenza, measles, and smallpox were previously unknown to Native Americans. With no natural immunity to such diseases, millions of American Indians died when exposed to them. Whole villages were wiped out as the illnesses spread by human contact between Native Americans and the new immigrants from Europe and Africa. An English colonist wrote in his diary, "[Indians] died on heapes, as they lay in their houses; and the living, that were able to shift for themselves, would runne away and let them dy, and let their Carkases ly above the ground without burial."

Despite the enormous problems both sides faced, they traded with

An illustration from a 1618 book by a Virginia settler shows two Native Americans "sitting at meate" and depicts some of the foods eaten by natives in the area, including fish, squid, nuts, and corn. Native advice on which foods to eat and their preparation was essential for the survival of Europeans.

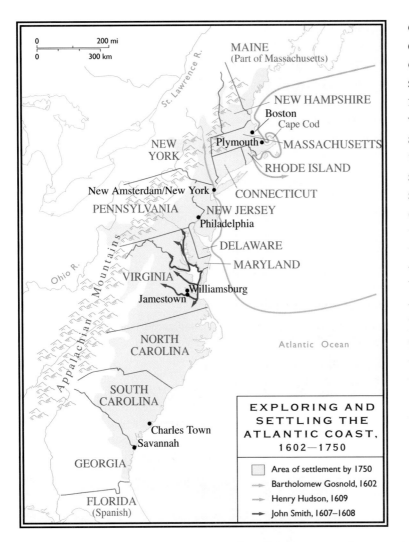

EXPLORING AND
SETTLING THE
ATLANTIC COAST,
1602—1750

Area of settlement by 1750
Bartholomew Gosnold, 1602
Henry Hudson, 1609
John Smith, 1607–1608

one another. The Europeans depended on the Native Americans for supplies of food such as corn and berries. The natives, on the other hand, were eager to trade their furs and food for copper pots and things made of iron and steel such as knives and axes. The settlers had come with the hope of developing trade. And trade they did. Like oil companies today, the colonial companies were multinational, supported by private investors. They were often forced to set up in hostile environments and to negotiate with foreign governments for rights to local resources. In colonial America, tensions often broke out during these "negotiations" when the Europeans attempted to take what they wanted by force.

Despite all the environmental hardships and the need to negotiate continuously with Native Americans, English and other European settlers continued to come to America. Tens of thousands of settlers, religious refugees, indentured servants, and convicts flooded to the New World. They came to make a new life—build businesses, practice their crafts. Companies were drawn to the New World for the trade— there was money to be made. The Plimouth Company established its colony in 1620 in what is now Plymouth, Massachusetts, and 10 years later, the Massachusetts Bay Company established another colony that eventually became the city of Boston. Dozens of other settlements sprang up in North America as well during the 17th century.

Investors formed more companies, built more ships, and hired more sailors to trade in the New World. The Dutch organized a new trading company, the Dutch West India Company, in 1623. The Dutch settlement at the southern tip of Manhattan was called New Amsterdam. We now call it New York City. The company purchased the whole island of Manhattan from the American Indians in 1626 for 60 guilders, or 24 dollars.

As the 17th century wore on, the English became more and more dominant. In a 1667 peace treaty, the Dutch gave New Netherland to the English. In 1673, the Dutch recaptured New Netherland only to surrender it again a year later. The entire Dutch colony later became the Colony of New York under the British. With this conquest, virtually the entire east coast of North America, from Georgia to Maine, was under the control of English settlers and British colonial authorities.

Yet there was still a vast region not under British control. It ran along the Ohio and Mississippi rivers, northward along the St. Lawrence River to Canada. This was an area rich in wildlife, dominated by the French and Native Americans who trapped and traded furs. Englishmen in New England began attacking the French settlers along the coast from northern Maine to Cape Breton Island in Canada. Although

A 1664 view of New Amsterdam, at the tip of Manhattan island, shows a prosperous Dutch settlement. A few years later, New Amsterdam, which was part of the colony of New Netherland, would be in the hands of the English, who later changed its name to New York.

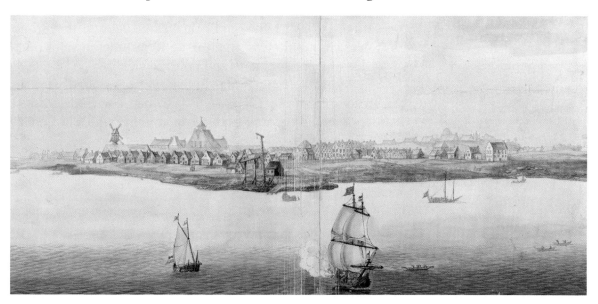

Reflecting the beaver's importance to the economy of New Netherland, a Dutch artist included a painting of one of the animals in a book about the natural wonders of North America. The beaver was prized for its thick fur, which was sold and made into coats and hats.

the French settlers were not numerous, they had alliances with Native Americans all across the inner regions that stretched from Maine and Canada down the St. Lawrence River valley to the Mississippi. Battles broke out between the British and French troops, while American Indians attacked English settlements. In this way, the stage was set for what became known as the French and Indian War, or the Seven Years' War. At that time the two world powers, England and France, were also engaged in a larger international war in parts of India, China, the Middle East, South America, and the Caribbean Islands.

In North America the British were determined to defeat the French and their Native American allies, and to expand British domination. In 1754 the British Lieutenant Governor of Virginia, Robert Dinwiddie, appointed 22-year-old George Washington as commander of the British troops and dispatched him to an important site located on the Ohio River at today's Pittsburgh. He was to build a fort and combat the French. But the French had already built a fort there. Nearby, Washington hastily built what he called Fort Necessity, but he and the fort were soon overwhelmed by French troops. That was not surprising, considering that Fort Necessity was not much of a fort. It looked more like a circle of sticks—not much protection for Washington's soldiers. Despite this and other early defeats, the British forces went on to win the war, and Washington went on to a distinguished military and political career.

When the French and Indian war concluded with the Treaty of Paris in 1763, the British had consolidated their dominion all the way from Georgia in the south to Canada in the north.

HELP WANTED: SLAVES

As the colonies expanded in the New World, it became clear that one major resource was seriously lacking—labor. The Europeans needed a workforce. The southern colonies were growing rice, sugarcane, tobacco, and cotton. The demand for labor became intense. With the Native Americans dying from diseases the Europeans had brought with them, the colonists looked elsewhere. Africans had been traded as slaves in Africa, the Middle East, and Europe for centuries. Until the mid-17th century, Portugal had a monopoly on the slave trade from Africa. In the 18th century, England took the lead. The English slave trade was a triangular route from England to the coast of Africa, from Africa to the New World, and then from the New World back to England. English slave traders brought beads, brandy, horses, cloth, and guns to the coast of Africa. They swapped these goods with African chiefs and middlemen for slaves. The slaves were then transported by ship to the New World, on the leg of the triangle known as the middle passage. On the final leg of the trade triangle, merchants returned to Europe with their cargo holds filled, not with humans, but with the fruits of slave labor—cotton, sugar, tobacco, molasses, and rum.

One of the most vivid portrayals of the middle passage is provided by Olaudah Equiano in *The Interesting Narrative of the Life of Olaudah Equiano.* Equiano's account of his capture

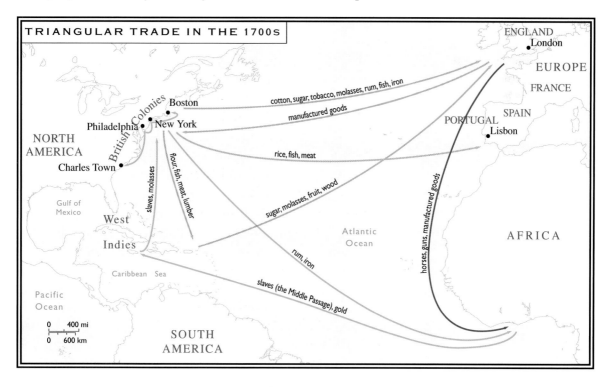

TRIANGULAR TRADE IN THE 1700s

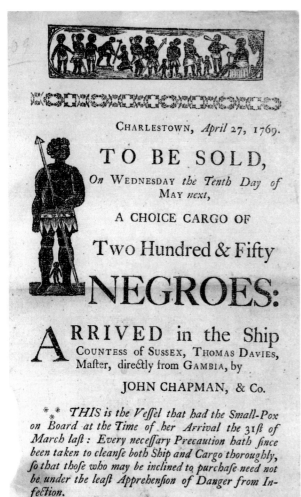

CHARLESTOWN, *April* 27, 1769.

TO BE SOLD,

On WEDNESDAY *the Tenth Day of* MAY *next,*

A CHOICE CARGO OF

Two Hundred & Fifty

NEGROES:

ARRIVED in the Ship COUNTESS of SUSSEX, THOMAS DAVIES, Mafter, directly from GAMBIA, by

JOHN CHAPMAN, & Co.

** THIS is the Veffel that had the Small-Pox on Board at the Time of her Arrival the 31ft of March laft: Every neceffary Precaution hath fince been taken to cleanfe both Ship and Cargo thoroughly, fo that thofe who may be inclined to purchafe need not be under the leaft Apprehenfion of Danger from Infection.

The NEGROES are allowed to be the likelieft Parcel that have been imported this Seafon.

A 1769 broadside, or flyer, from Charlestown (now Charleston), South Carolina, advertises a new shipment of slaves from the African nation of Gambia. A note at the bottom reassures potential buyers that the human cargo is free of the dreaded and highly contagious disease of smallpox.

and enslavement in Africa and his horrific experiences aboard a slave ship bound for the West Indies shocked his readers and became one of the most effective antislavery accounts of its time. In 1789, after he bought his own freedom, he wrote this autobiography. Some say Equiano pieced together the stories of others and made them his own, while others say it was Equiano's story alone, but all agree that from his book, we get an accurate picture of how the slave trade shattered human life.

According to his story, Equiano, the 11-year-old son of an African chief, was kidnapped in 1755 by slave traders from his home along the Niger River. He was supposed to have followed in his father's footsteps and become a village elder, a judge, and a chief. Instead, he was one of the 6 million Africans transported during the 18th century.

Six or seven months after being kidnapped, Equiano arrived at the coast of Africa, where the Europeans had built forts for trading posts. There he saw his first slave ship. As he described it, "The first object which saluted my eyes when I arrived on the coast was the sea, and a slave ship, which was then riding at anchor and waiting for its cargo." The cargo was human. Equiano was carried on board and inspected to see if he was healthy. Equiano couldn't understand the foreigners. He didn't speak their language and they didn't speak his. That only added to his terror. He wrote, "When I looked round the ship too, and saw... a multitude of black people of every description chained together, every one of their countenances expressing dejection and sorrow." He was sure at that point he would be killed. Later, he wished that he had been. He related, "I was soon put down under the decks, and there I received such a... loathsomeness of the stench...

I became so sick and low that I was not able to eat, nor had I the least desire to taste anything." The slave traders packed the Africans in so tight that the slaves could not stand up, or even turn around. The foul air rose to such temperatures many fainted, and just as many died. Equiano lay in the suffocating heat listening to the "shrieks of the women and the groans of the dying."

The middle passage normally took 60 to 90 days, but it could take as long as four months. Day after day, week after week, month after month, they were crammed like cattle in the hold, until many preferred to throw themselves overboard than endure another day. Equiano noted that "two of my wearied countrymen who were chained together...jumped into the sea....I believe many more would very soon have done the same if they had not been prevented by the ship's crew."

When the ships landed in the New World, the merchants wasted no time selling their "goods." They led the slaves into a yard, in Equiano's words, "like so many sheep in a fold," and then, "[o]n a signal given (as the beat of a drum) the buyers rush at once into the yard where the slaves are confined and make choice of that parcel they like best." Equiano was shipped to an English colony in Virginia, where he was purchased by a lieutenant in the Royal Navy. He was, like merchandise, part of a trade. But back home, alongside the Niger River, his family remembered him. They chanted these words,

> Who are we looking for, who are we looking for?
> It's Equiano we're looking for.
> Has he gone to the stream? Let him come back.
> Has he gone to the farm? Let him return.
> It's Equiano we're looking for."

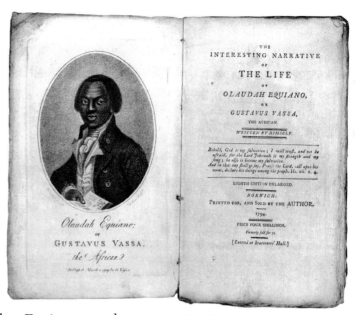

Former slave Olaudah Equiano published his autobiography in 1789, after he had purchased his own freedom and moved to England. The book was a best-seller, and Equiano became wealthy as a result. He also became active in the abolitionist movement in England, which worked to outlaw slavery.

The Horror of the Middle Passage

ALEXANDER FALCONBRIDGE, AN ACCOUNT OF THE SLAVE TRADE ON THE COAST OF AFRICA, 1792

Alexander Falconbridge served as surgeon on slave ships during the 18th century. He witnessed first-hand the slave trade. These excerpts from Falconbridge's book An Account of the Slave Trade on the Coast of Africa, *published in 1792, detail the second leg of the English trade triangle—the middle passage, the journey from West Africa to the West Indies.*

From the time of the arrival of the ships to their departure, which is usually near three months, scarce a day passes without some Negroes being purchased, and carried on board.... The men Negroes, on being brought aboard the ship, are immediately fastened together, two and two, by handcuffs on their wrists and by irons riveted on their legs....

Upon the Negroes refusing to take sustenance, I have seen coals of fire, glowing hot, put on a shovel and placed so near their lips as to scorch and burn them. And this has been accompanied with threats of forcing them to swallow the coals if they... persisted in refusing to eat.... the floor of their rooms, was so covered with the blood and mucus... from... the flux [diarrhea], that it resembled a slaughter-house. It is not in the power of the human imagination to picture a situation more dreadful or disgusting....

The place allotted for the sick Negroes is under the half deck, where they lie on the bare planks.... those who are emaciated frequently have their skin and even their flesh entirely rubbed off, by the motion of the ship, from the prominent parts of the shoulders, elbows and hips so as to render the bones quite bare. The excruciating pain which the poor sufferers feel from being obliged to continue in such a dreadful situation, frequently for several weeks, in case they happen to live so long....

Various deceptions... in the disposal [sale] of sick slaves... must excite in every humane mind the liveliest sensations of horror. I have been well informed that a Leverpool captain boasted of his having cheated some Jews by the following stratagem. A lot of slaves afflicted with the flux, being about to be landed for sale, he directed the ship's surgeons to stop the anus of each of them with oakum...the bargain was struck and the slaves were accordingly sold....But it was not long before discovery ensued. The excruciating pain...not being able to be borne by the poor wretches, the temporary obstruction was removed and the deluded purchasers were speedily convinced of the imposition."

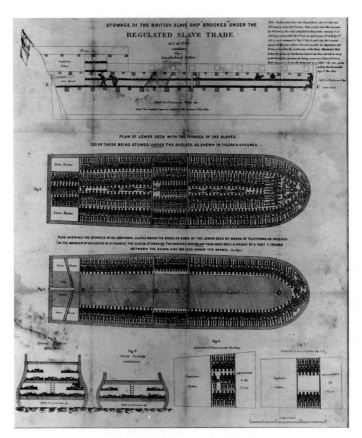

A plan of the lower deck of the English slave ship Brookes shows how its human cargo was arranged on two levels during transport to America. To fit the maximum number of slaves on the ship, 6-feet-wide platforms were built between the floor and ceiling of the deck, and slaves were laid side by side on both levels, without enough headroom to sit up. Such illustrations were used by abolitionist groups to publicize the cruelty of slavery.

CHAPTER 2

RUDE AWAKENINGS
WEALTH REDEFINED

In 1735, king Philip V of Spain approved a joint French and Spanish scientific expedition to Peru. The mission, which 21-year-old naval officer Antonio De Ulloa chose to accept, was to measure a segment of the meridian, a north-south circle around the earth that goes through the poles, at the equator. Through careful measurements, the scientists hoped to determine the exact size and shape of the earth. For more than a decade De Ulloa and the other scientists on the expedition explored the Amazon, conducting scientific experiments with clocks and barometers and collecting bugs and plants. De Ulloa took careful notes for his report to the king. While recording his scientific observations, he included his observations of life in Peru, and what he saw disturbed him.

Antonio De Ulloa's account of his expedition to Peru in the 1730s included illustrations of the lush natural surroundings. It also contained harrowing descriptions of the mills and mines where native Peruvians were forced to toil in dangerous conditions.

The economic system in Peru depended on forced labor. Spanish law required the natives to work for the Spaniards under conditions that amounted to slavery. De Ulloa described a typical work day in the textile mills: "work…begins before dawn…the workshop overseer locks the doors, leaving the Indians imprisoned in the room." The quotas that the overseers demanded of the workers, who were chained to their looms, was often more than could be accomplished in a day—even the long work days that began and ended in the dark. If the quotas weren't met, the natives were whipped mercilessly—hundreds of strokes. Whippings weren't the only abuse the natives faced. Local officials demanded the natives keep their hair long so that authorities could tie them by their hair to horses' tails and drag them to work. As horrible as De Ulloa's accounts sounded, the conditions in the

Peruvian silver mines were even worse. And perhaps the worst of them all was *Cerro Ricco*—Rich Mountain.

Hundreds of thousands of natives died on that bitterly cold mountain peak from exposure to the elements, from disease, from mining accidents, and from the brutality of their masters. Natives chewed coca leaves to dull their hunger pains. Small children were sent squirreling through mine passages too small for adults. Others were sent into the mines to test the air. If they came back, the air was breathable; if not...In return, *Cerro Ricco* gave up 25,000 tons of silver—more than half the world's production of silver. It produced enough silver to fund an empire, enough silver to build a Spanish fleet. So much silver poured from *Cerro Ricco* that the streets of the mining town, Potosì, were said to have been paved with silver bars. Spain was rich and getting richer. Silver was pouring in from the Spanish colonies in the New World.

It wasn't just precious metals that were valuable. After finding the "Spice Islands" of the Moluccas just east of Indonesia in the 16th century, traders began chasing cloves, nutmeg, mace, and cinnamon. Dutch traders especially imported great quantities of these rare spices. What made them rare was the fact that they did not grow in Europe. The limited supply made for a very high demand. A shipowner importing these spices to Europe could make a profit of 15 to 20 or even 100 times their cost. Visions of astronomical profits from all these natural resources lured merchants and adventurers into making the very risky trips across the vast oceans to the New World or to southeast Asia in search of riches. An English pamphlet published at the time reported, "The undoubted Interest of England is Trade, since it is that alone which can make us either *Rich* or *Safe,* for without a powerful Navy, we should be prey to our Neighbors, and without Trade, we could have neither sea-men [n]or Ships."

An ornate silver tray made in Alto Peru (today's Bolivia) shows floral designs and a figure thought to be St. John the Baptist. The religious theme reflects the influence of the Spanish, who controlled the area and its great wealth of silver mines during the 16th, 17th, and 18th centuries.

By the time this view of the British East India Company's London home was painted in the mid-18th century, the location was known as Old East India wharf. It had been a bustling departure and arrival point for ships carrying goods for trade for more than 100 years.

This was the age of mercantilism, when governments attempted to increase the wealth of their countries by regulating and even sponsoring commerce and foreign trade.

THE COMPANY YOU KEEP

Governments had two primary goals. The first was to acquire gold. National business leaders believed that precious metals made a nation rich. The more gold and silver in the treasury, the richer the nation—or so they thought. The second goal was to create rules and regulations so that their country sold more to other countries than they bought—to export as much as possible and import as little as possible. Instead of entering into free trade with merchants from other countries, merchants and political leaders came up with new trading devices called "trading companies."

The state-sponsored British East India Company was founded in 1600. It was started by a group of merchants who proposed working together to do business in India. Almost at the same time, Dutch businessmen with the same idea created the Dutch East India Company. This company sponsored Henry Hudson's trip to the New World and his discovery of the Hudson River. Another trading company, the Dutch West India Company, founded in 1623, established New Netherland in America the following year. These and other companies set out to establish more colonies and trade posts.

The main purpose of trading companies was to create monopolies for overseas trade—especially over precious goods such as gold, silver, and spices. Greedy traders constantly took wealth, territory—and ships—by force. Piracy broke out everywhere. Only the presence of large naval fleets could control this chaos of semi-legal bounty hunting.

The word *pirate* brings the image of a scoundrel with an eye patch and a wooden leg, complete with a parrot sitting on his shoulder. But the pirates sacking trade ships were aboard other trade ships. Queen Elizabeth established some colonies in the Americas as naval bases for the purpose of piracy. One purpose of the failed Roanoke colony, established by the British in 1585 in Virginia, was to attack Spanish ships laden with treasure. No one was safe, including Antonio De Ulloa, whose frigate the *Déliverance* was attacked on his return to Spain. The *Déliverance* was captured by the British navy, which confiscated De Ulloa's scientific papers and took De Ulloa prisoner. Fortunately, De Ulloa's data from his time in South America was so valued he was welcomed in the English scientific community and eventually released.

"*Th*[e] division of labor, from which so many advantages are derived, is not originally the effect of any human wisdom. . . . It is the necessary. . . consequence of a certain propensity in human nature. . . . the propensity to truck, barter, and exchange one thing for another."

—Adam Smith, *The Wealth of Nations*, 1776

Merchant ships, which carried out the business of the British East India Company, are featured prominently on the company's coat of arms, which is similar to a company logo of today. This coat of arms, used until 1709, represented a very successful company that made its investors rich.

Each European nation had to maintain a naval fleet to protect its merchant ships from piracy by other nations. The mercantilist philosophy led to war among the European states, each desperate to gain control over natural riches—gold, silver, spices. The British, Dutch, French, and Spanish navies fought each other around the world. The Dutch and English battled continuously during the 17th and 18th centuries for control of the shipping lanes in the English Channel, which connected the North Sea and Spain and the Mediterranean. If they couldn't cross the Channel, ships would have to travel all the way around England.

In the summer of 1588, Philip II, the king of Spain, prepared for war against England to gain control of the English Channel. He ordered builders to convert his merchant ships into warships. Smaller ships were outfitted for use by messengers and spies. In July, the Spanish fleet—the Great Armada—advanced on the English ships in the English Channel. They tried to get close enough to throw their grappling irons onto the English decks and draw them in tight so the Spanish soldiers could swing on board with swords drawn for hand-to-hand combat. But the faster,

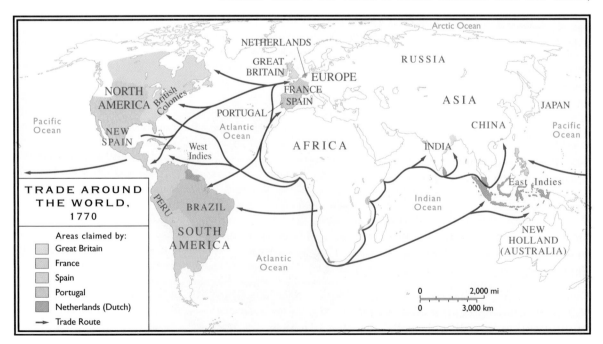

more agile English ships kept out of range and used their cannons to punch holes in the Spanish hulls. The Spanish seamen worked to exhaustion to bail out the water, but the pumps could not keep three of the Spanish ships afloat and they sank to the bottom. The rest of the fleet limped away through the shallows, and when the wind shifted to the southwest they ran with it, out of the grasp of the English. But luck was not with them. The Armada was scattered by storms. What the English didn't sink, the sea took. The defeat was devastating. Later, the English sarcastically referred to the Great Armada as the "Invincible" Armada.

The English Channel wasn't the only place sea battles were being fought. In Asia, the Portuguese, Dutch, and English navies fought for control of Malaysia, the Indonesian islands, and India. In the new colonies of

A Spanish ship explodes during a battle with the Dutch fleet in the Bay of Gibraltar in April 1607, sending sailors and supplies flying in every direction. European powers were constantly battling each other to control shipping and trade during the 17th and 18th centuries.

America, the English created regulations that excluded the Dutch from trading with the colonies. With all this fighting going on, it was clear mercantilism was not working.

AN INVISIBLE HAND

War wasn't the only fallout from following mercantilist policies. With so much gold available, merchants could charge almost any price for their wares—and the prices of merchandise soared. Things were costing more—a *lot* more. The wealthiest landowners were making only a fraction of what merchants were pulling in. Times were changing. Some nobles could no longer pay their bills and were forced to sell their estates—homes and land that had been in their families for generations. The farmers working for the nobles on these estates found their lives changed as well. They may not have had a glamorous life, but at least they had a roof over their heads, and even when times got bad they could count on a small share of the estate's grain and livestock to put food on the table. Now they would have to scramble for work. And what if there were no jobs?

These were the problems that the great minds of the early 18th century debated. How could people create economic prosperity for society as a whole and the household goods that everyone needed and still make a good profit? One particularly brilliant thinker wrote near the end of the 18th century about his own philosophy of economics. Today, he is still considered one of the most brilliant economists ever and the founder of modern economics. His name, like his life, was rather ordinary—Adam Smith.

Adam Smith could have been the model for the "absent-minded-professor" stereotype. He walked with a peculiar stumbling step, lurching about as if the act of putting one foot in front of the other took too much away from his deep thoughts. Once he was so focused on an academic discussion that he fell right into a pit.

Smith was a quiet, studious person who lived a quiet, studious life. The most remarkable event in his unadventurous life (other than falling into the pit) happened when

Adam Smith wrote one of the most influential works on economics the world has seen, The Wealth of Nations. *Smith thought it was basic human nature for people to trade with each other. He called this "the propensity to truck, barter, and exchange one thing for another," and he felt that it benefited everyone.*

The Paradoxes of Hard Work and Riches

" **JOHN WESLEY, "THOUGHTS UPON METHODISM," AUGUST 4, 1786**

The 15th child of a minister, John Wesley studied at Oxford University before becoming a preacher in the Church of England in 1728. He and his brother participated in a religious study group nicknamed the "Methodists" for its methodical approach to study. In a letter to the leader of another congregation, Wesley wrote of his concern that leading a dedicated life of working hard and saving money would lead to an increase in an individual's wealth. The accumulation of wealth would lead people to buy things, and owning and enjoying worldly things would make them less religious. Thus, Wesley cautioned, wealth was a threat to religion.

John Wesley was the founder of a branch of Protestantism called Methodism. He feared the corrupting effects of money and once said, "When I have money, I get rid of it quickly, lest it find a way into my heart."

I fear, wherever riches have increased, the essence of religion has decreased, in the same proportion. Therefore, I do not see how it is possible, in the nature of things, for any true revival of religion to continue long. For religion must necessarily produce both industry and frugality, and these cannot but produce riches. But as riches increase, so will pride, anger, and love of the world in all its branches. How then is it possible that Methodism, that is, a religion of the heart, though it flourishes now as a green bay tree, should continue in this state? For the Methodists in every place grow diligent and frugal; consequently they increase in goods. Hence they proportionately increase in pride, in anger, in the desire of the flesh, the desire of the eyes, and the pride of life. So, although the form of religion remains, the spirit is swiftly vanishing away. Is there no way to prevent this—this continual decay of pure religion? We ought not to prevent people from being diligent and frugal; we must exhort all Christians to gain all they can and to save all they can; that is, in effect to grow rich.

> "Whatever a person saves from his revenue he adds to his capital, and either employs it himself in maintaining an additional number of productive hands, or enables some other person to do so, by lending it to him for an interest, that is, for a share of the profits."
>
> —Adam Smith, *The Wealth of Nations*, 1776

he was just four years old. He was kidnapped by a band of gypsies passing through his hometown of Kirkcaldy in Scotland. Poor little Adam couldn't have been particularly entertaining, because the gypsies tired of him in just a few hours and let him go.

Although Smith may not have been dashing and daring (he was rather homely, in fact), he was an excellent student. In 1739, when he was 16, the precocious youth was awarded a scholarship to Oxford University. At the time, Oxford encouraged students to read widely—so long as they steered clear of any "dangerous" books. Adam Smith came close to getting expelled for reading David Hume's *Treatise of Human Nature*—a book now considered a masterpiece of philosophy but back then was considered dangerous. It was dangerous because Hume argued against the Christian belief in miracles. He claimed, "A miracle is a violation of the laws of nature." Religious leaders and the general public did not look kindly on such attacks on Christianity.

After graduating from Oxford in 1751, Smith was appointed professor at the University of Glasgow, where he taught moral philosophy for many years. He eventually retired and wrote the book that made him famous, *The Wealth of Nations*. It was published in 1776—the same year as the Declaration of Independence was written. Many people today argue about which work was more important— the Declaration of Independence, which announced to the world the birth of a new society, or *The Wealth of Nations*, which outlined for the world how to make that society work economically.

In *The Wealth of Nations,* Smith argued that trade between nations, rather than rewarding only the trader, in fact benefits both parties. Both buyer and seller benefit from the freedom of exchange. Rather than restricting markets, he argued, the buying and selling of things ought to be open to everyone, which would encourage more businessmen to start up new businesses and bring more goods to the market.

This raised another problem for Smith. If merchants intend to make money or "to better their condition," as Smith put it, what prevents them from ripping off the buyer?

Smith's answer was *competition*. If you wanted to sell your bicycle, for example, you are not going to get 100 million dollars for it. In fact, if you tried to charge even a little more than what bicycles were selling for down the block, your bicycle would rust before you would pocket any money on its sale. So it goes for all the players in the business world. If you are looking for a job and demand more than everyone else, you're not going to find work. If you have a job you want done and you're not willing to pay the going rate, who are you going to get to do it? Competition prevents the greedy from getting away with exploiting others—as if, as Smith claims, an "Invisible Hand" keeps us honest.

It was also during this time in England that the manufacturing of cotton and woolen textiles rapidly increased. Businessmen from the cities organized weavers in the countryside to work for them at home. The merchants brought the cloth produced by the weavers to market in distant cities. Soon the invention of mechanical spinning and weaving devices made this process more profitable. By bringing the workers, the raw materials, and the machines together in one place, a factory was born—another step

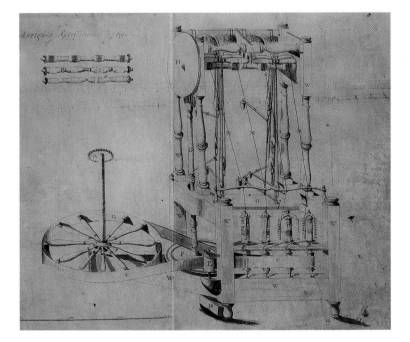

The English barber Richard Arkwright made improvements to the "spinning jenny," a machine that turned cotton into yarn. The wheel on the left, probably powered by water, turns a belt that turns the gears, rods, and spindles in the complex spinning mechanism on the right. The cotton was placed at the top back of the machine, spun into thread, and wound onto the spools at the bottom front. Arkwright was also the first to use the latest technology in the 1760s, the steam engine, in the manufacture of textiles.

toward efficient manufacturing. In *The Wealth of Nations*, Smith talked about how workers carried out their jobs in this new manufacturing process. He used a pin factory as his example: "One man draws out the wire, another straits it, a third cuts it, a fourth points it, a fifth grinds it at the top for receiving the head."

Early in the 18th century another invention appeared on the scene—the steam engine, a new kind of engine that converted heat energy into mechanical energy. The heat energy was supplied by burning wood or coal. The heat boiled water, which then gave off steam. The steam provided the mechanical energy necessary to push pistons in the engine. Initially these steam engines were used to pump water from mines. Workers were able to go deeper into mine shafts and could produce more coal. It wasn't long before engines were used to power machinery and boats for river transportation.

The Spanish, among others, overlooked this efficient process of manufacturing. The Spanish seemed blind to their own economic decline. They thought they were the richest people on the earth because they had so much gold. They thought that they did not have to work hard to produce wealth, to make their country prosperous. One rich Spaniard in the mid-17th century rather flippantly dismissed the idea of Spain developing its own industry, saying, "Let London manufacture those fabrics of hers to her heart's content; Holland her chambrays; Florence her cloth; the Indies their beaver and vicuna; Milan her brocades...so long as our capital can enjoy them."

But others were not so blind. A Moroccan ambassador visiting Madrid in the 1690s saw that the great wealth of the

"It is not from the benevolence of the butcher, the brewer, or the baker, that we expect our dinner, but from their regard to their own interest."

—Adam Smith, *The Wealth of Nations*, 1776

Spanish came from treasure imported from the New World—not from hard work and the manufacturing of goods. He recognized that this enjoyment of luxury was connected to a dislike of handicrafts and the rejection of manual work. He wrote, "handicrafts practiced by the lower classes and common people are despised by this nation... those who practice these crafts in Spain are Frenchmen [who] flock to Spain to look for work."

In contrast to the Spanish rejection of manual work and their dependence on imported silver, English inventors were putting themselves to work during this time inventing the new steam engine. Many improvements were made on the steam engine throughout the 18th century. By the end of the century steam engines were used to power machinery used in the manufacturing process described by Adam Smith. This made the English economy and others that used the new manufacturing techniques much more efficient. On the other hand, without innovative businessmen and a skilled local labor force, the Spanish economy virtually collapsed.

With the inexpensive manufacturing processes emerging in England, Holland, and elsewhere came *stuff*—shoes, hats, belts, furniture, cloth, pottery, nails, sewing pins— things that until now only the privileged could purchase. With the harnessing of steam energy to run machines, the whole process became even more efficient. And in the midst of all this activity were people—people working hard in a disciplined way, rather than wasting time or effort on unproductive activities. Such industriousness, according to Adam Smith, was the real basis of wealth, not gold or silver piling up in a treasury.

Isabel de Borbon was the wife of Spain's King Felipe IV. In the 1630s her portrait was painted by Diego Velázquez, perhaps the greatest Spanish painter of his time. Isabel's clothing, made from splendid fabrics that were probably imported, reflects the riches enjoyed by Spanish nobility in the 17th century.

CHAPTER 3

MOST MAGNIFICENT
THE OTTOMAN EMPIRE

Imagine that you are a 12-year-old boy living in the Ottoman Empire—centered in today's Turkey—more than 500 years ago. Perhaps your family was Albanian and had fled into the rocky hillsides to escape from the Ottoman Turks. By the evening fire, you hear the stories whispered. Everyone's favorite is the one about Skanderbeg, Albania's magnificent hero. Skanderbeg kept the Ottoman sultan's best soldiers at bay. The Ottoman Turks attacked the hillsides 24 times, and 24 times they failed. But as in all good stories, there is a part that frightens you—it makes your heart beat faster, and you sometimes have to remember to breathe. It's what happened to Skanderbeg when he was your age—and in fact happens to many boys your age—that scares you the most.

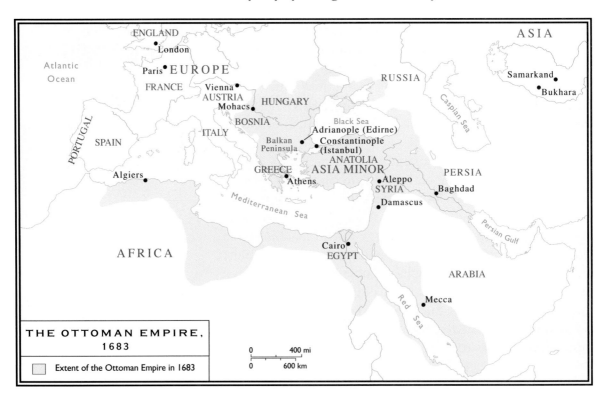

THE OTTOMAN EMPIRE,
1683

Extent of the Ottoman Empire in 1683

No one says the word in your earshot, but somehow you know it. It's *devshirme*—the Turkish word meaning "collection." Young boys—Christians, Jews, and others who were not Muslim—were taken from their families throughout the empire. The Ottomans knew parents would behave if their children were held hostage. Every three or four years the collectors came, especially to the Balkan countries of Bosnia, Albania, Macedonia, Greece, and Bulgaria. In the early 1600s the sultan took as many as 2,000 boys between the ages of 10 and 14. Christians and Jews in the Ottoman Empire were given protected status because they were "people of the book"—believers in the Bible or the Jewish Torah. They were allowed to live freely and follow their religious beliefs as long as they paid a heavy tax. But the Ottomans did not extend that protection to young males; they were instead "tribute children," children gathered up as tribute, or payment, to the sultan.

Once the young boys were collected, they were inspected for physical perfection and later quizzed to determine how smart they were. Some of the boys were taken to the homes of peasants, where they were taught Turkish ways and the practice of Islam. Others, like Skanderbeg, joined the soldiers in military barracks for army training. If the Ottoman officials thought that a particular boy was very smart, he would be sent to the school within the sacred confines of the sultan's grand palace. These boys were the lucky ones. They entered royal service, attended the Imperial Palace School, and received an excellent education. This is what happened to Lufti Pasha and Kochu Bey, two young boys who lived about a hundred years apart. Both were born in the Balkans, and after converting to Islam they were placed in royal service.

The interior of Topkapi Palace in Istanbul was ornate and sumptuous, befitting the sultans who lived there.

Learning to read was an important part of the young pages' training in the grand palace in Istanbul. The palace school was unique in the history of the Muslim world—it was unusual for young people to learn to read and write either Arabic or Turkish. Most Muslims simply memorized a few verses of the Quran, the sacred book of Islam.

In his autobiography, Lufti Pasha described his early life in the palace in the 16th century, where he "was brought up in the Sultan's Private Apartments through the bounty of the Sultan... When I was in the Private apartments, I studied many kinds of science." When Kochu Bey entered royal service in the first decade of the 17th century, hundreds of "pages," or messengers and errand boys who were slaves, lived in the quarters of the grand palace in Istanbul. They were required to perform all kinds of duties, such as carrying messages to officials or delivering food from the kitchens to the sultan, or to his wives and family living in the palace. The pages were sworn never to mention anything they saw in the palace, or they would be killed.

We know much about their daily life thanks to one Polish page named Bobovi, a Christian who had been captured and enslaved in the 1630s. He did not keep silent. He wrote an unauthorized report about "everything [that it is] possible to learn about what happens in the Palace." He had converted to Islam and served as a court musician for 19 years before being dismissed for bad behavior. After his release from the palace he revealed what he knew about palace life. He hoped to clear up "events and palace affairs which foreigners have only spoken about in a confused and uncertain way up to now."

According to Bobovi, the pages' training lasted for about seven years. After learning Turkish and some Arabic, they were taught to memorize and recite the Quran, the sacred book of Islam. The goal was almost philosophical, Bobovi explained: "The sultan's intention is not to make them great scholars and not to demand of them anything more than a great respect for books and especially for the Quran." What the pages learned depended on their own interests and skills, and was not entirely focused on Islamic subjects. Unlike the schooling in the Islamic colleges outside, which emphasized the Quran, palace training was very practical, designed to make the boys useful in the Ottoman administration.

The Imperial Palace School prepared its students for particular professions, such as becoming a *katib*, a professional secretary. This was a position of honor and respect throughout the empire. The *katib* could read and write. Imagine how important that made him among those who were illiterate—which was nearly everybody else.

These young men, trained to read and write and in the arts of governing, became ministers of state, governors of provinces, and military commanders. They received additional training in archery, horsemanship, wrestling, and javelin throwing. Likewise, the Palace School opened doors for young men to become tax collectors, experts who ran state offices, and even governors of whole provinces. If a young man in royal service wanted to study Islamic law and its teachings, he could become the leader of a royal mosque. Royal mosque leaders were paid well and received gifts from the congregation and the sultan. Or a page could study Islamic law and became a judge.

The boys who were fortunate enough to study in the palace school could advance to ever-higher positions. Lufti

The elite soldiers of the Ottoman Empire, called Janissaries, often wore elaborate uniforms. This officer, with his plumed headdress, must have held a very high rank, and he would have stood out from the rest of his men. The dagger in his belt signifies that he is a warrior, and his red boots have the pointed toe of the Arab style.

"*From* the time that they first enter the school of the Grand Seraglio [palace] they are exceedingly well-directed. Day by day they are continuously instructed in good and comely behavior, in the discipline of the senses, in military prowess, and in a knowledge of the Moslem faith; in a word, in all the virtues of mind and body."

—Ottaviano Bon, Venetian diplomat, in *The Palace of the Grand Sultan*, 1608

Pasha described his rise in the palace ranks, "I graduated from the post of Cloth-Bearer [a person who brings the sultan drinks and clothes], to become Muteferrika [palace guard]... Then I was Head Taster, then Head Gatekeeper and then Master of the Standard [caretaker of the flags and banners of the sultan's army]. Afterwards [I became] Governor... Then the vizierate [Grand Vizier]." The position of Grand Vizier was the most magnificent appointed office in the Ottoman Empire. Some of the Grand Viziers actually ruled the whole empire. It was this powerful position that Lufti Pasha held in the mid-16th century, and that Kochu Bey held in the early 17th century.

The collection system was designed to bring in fresh talent from outside the Islamic religion. Many Europeans admired it because it created wise and well-trained administrators instead of relying on untrained people the way most European governments did. "It is not astonishing that the Turkish nation prospers," wrote a French historian at the time, "since the Turks know so well how to choose the *elite* from the great number of youths and how to give them the instruction."

EDUCATION OUTSIDE THE PALACE WALLS

Islamic education outside the sultan's palace was very different. It was focused on learning the Quran and what the great Islamic scholars had to say about it. It was not focused on practical ends such as a career in government service or diplomacy, but on religious learning and perfection. The Quran says, "We have sent down to thee the Book, explaining all things," and "We have ignored nothing in the Book." Muslims believed that knowledge of this book was absolutely essential, both for this life and for the hereafter. It provided indispensable knowledge about proper daily conduct and promised to show the way to paradise in the afterlife. The Islamic scholars believed that they had received from God a perfect book, full of wisdom. Students devoted great effort to memorizing the whole Quran. A person who successfully memorizes the Quran, with perfect pronunciation, is called a *Hafiz,* an Arabic word meaning "to protect," "to preserve," or "to memorize," and so, *Hafiz* is one "who memorizes the Quran."

Although many Islamic scholars were good mathematicians, they did not formally study the natural sciences, such as biology, physics, and chemistry, or the "electrical" studies, which is what the Europeans called the study of electricity. Many Arabs and Muslims had a great interest in astronomy at this time because people judged time by the movement of the stars and planets and Islamic scholars wanted to know the time for prayers.

In the 1570s, Turkish astronomers and time-keepers had proposed the building of a new observatory in Istanbul in order to correct astronomical data from the past. But before construction could be completed, Islamic clergymen convinced the sultan to order the military to destroy the building. The clerics pointed out that no law of nature could violate Islamic law. At the time, astronomy and astrology were studied together, and astrology in particular was not accepted by Islamic thought. Astrology deals with predicting the future, a practice that contradicts Islamic belief, because only God knows what will happen.

These 17th-century tiles made by an Ottoman craftsman depict the Kaaba, the sacred Muslim shrine in Mecca (Saudi Arabia). The circular opening around the Kaaba represents the archway through which pilgrims pass on their journey into the space, where they walk seven times together around the shrine. Verses from the Quran appear on the top tiles.

SULTAN OF SULTANS

In the early 17th century, Kochu Bey was Grand Vizier. He recognized that the Ottoman Empire had begun to descend from its heights of glory. In his 1630 report to the sultan, he wrote honestly about the strengths and weaknesses of the Ottoman Empire: "It is a long time since the... household of the lofty Sultanate... was served by solicitous, well-intentioned, worthy ulema [religious scholars] and by obedient, self-effacing, willing slaves." Kochu Bey recognized that the sultanate needed to be reformed. He hoped to find the reasons for the decline and bring them to the sultan's attention.

Kochu Bey stressed the glories of Ottoman history, especially the achievements of the Sultan of Sultans, Suleiman

After a great fire destroyed nearly all of London in 1666, King Charles II commissioned architect Christopher Wren to rebuild the city's churches, including St. Paul's Cathedral. Wren's design for St. Paul's featured a large dome instead of the traditional tall steeple. Many critics disliked the dome because they thought it represented Catholic or Italian tastes. But the domed shape was a Middle Eastern invention that had come to Europe as early as the 13th century.

the Magnificent. Suleiman died in 1566, but he brought the Ottoman Empire to its greatest glory during his lifetime. Kochu Bey used Suleiman as an example of what the perfect sultan should be. The Quran identifies King Solomon as the perfect monarch because of his wisdom in applying justice to all, and Kochu Bey regarded Suleiman (named after the wise king) second only to Solomon for seeking justice.

In addition, Suleiman began a series of building projects that gave the Ottoman Empire its distinctive architectural style. The brilliant architect responsible for that style, arguably the most magnificent architect who ever lived, was named Sinan. He had also been brought into royal service through the collection system. Sultan Suleiman appointed Sinan head architect in 1538, and he designed or supervised the construction of hundreds of mosques, bridges, aqueducts, and other structures, many of which are still considered masterpieces of engineering and art.

Architects all over the world studied Sinan's work and the Ottomans' buildings. One British architect, Christopher Wren, became particularly fascinated by the Ottoman mosques. He became convinced that the European Gothic style of architecture had Muslim roots. Wren was so captivated by Muslim architecture that he used elements of it in his own designs. When Wren designed St. Paul's Cathedral in London in the 1660s and 1670s he used the combination of dome and tower that is typical of Muslim architecture and which had existed before the Islamic style.

The centerpiece of Muslim architecture is the mosque, with its large central dome. Within the mosque complex, under the dome, worshippers gather in a large, open space for prayer. This open space is a perfect cube. The length, width, and height to the top of the dome are of equal dimensions. A tall, slender tower on the side of the mosque called a minaret is designed so that the muezzin, the person calling others to prayer, could climb to the top and issue his call in all four directions of the compass. Inside the prayer hall is a prayer niche. Worshippers were expected to orient themselves toward this niche in the wall so that they would directly face Mecca, the holy city of Islam.

A magnificent example of this style of mosque complex is the great Suleimaniye mosque in Istanbul, built by Sinan between 1550 and 1557. It is actually a group of 14 buildings. The buildings are joined by a hospital, a place for people to stay overnight, a soup kitchen, and a communal bath. (The Turkish bath, as it was later known, was more than a place to wash up—it was a community gathering spot where people got together to celebrate weddings and births, mourn lost loved ones, and share daily news.)

The prayer hall is connected to a large room used as a mausoleum, or burial place, for Suleiman. Between the main buildings and the rest of the complex there is a garden. Travelers from the West admired such Ottoman gardens, not only for their individual flowers, such as the tulip and the iris, but also for their designs, which were copied for country houses all over Europe.

Western travelers' descriptions of Turkish baths sparked a trend back in Europe. Turkish baths became so popular in Europe they began popping up by the hundreds. One Scottish street in Glasgow, Bath Street, got its name from the baths built there. Europeans believed the baths cured everything

The Selimiye mosque in Erdirne (formerly Adrianople), Turkey, is a splendid example of the architecture of Sinan, who was commissioned by Suleiman the Magnificent to build it in the 16th century. The mosque's spacious design features a raised platform in the center from which the religious leader could address worshippers. Below it is a fountain that could be used by Muslims to wash themselves before prayers.

A Turkish woman, holding a metal bowl used for pouring water over the body, along with what may be a soap holder, is dressed for a day at the hammam, or baths. This elaborate ritual involved several pieces of equipment, including the special nalin, *or clogs, that were designed to keep the feet off the bath's wet floor.*

from gout to mental illness. As Lady Mary Wortley Montagu, wife of the British ambassador to the Ottoman Empire, reported in 1717:

In one of these cover'd Waggons I went to the Bagnio about 10 a clock. It was allready full of Women. It is built of Stone in the shape of a Dome with no Windows but in the Roofe, which gives Light enough. There was 5 of these domes joyn'd together, the outmost being less than the rest and serving only as a hall where the portress stood at the door. Ladys of Quality gennerally give this Woman the value of a crown or 10 shillings, and I did not forget that ceremony. The next room is a very large one, pav'd with Marble, and all round it rais'd 2 Sofas of marble, one above another. There were 4 fountains of cold Water in this room, falling first into marble Basins and then running on the floor in little channels made for that purpose, which carry'd the streams into the next room, something less than this, with the same sort of marble sofas, but so hot with steams of sulphur proceeding from the baths joyning to it, twas impossible to stay there with one's Cloths on. The 2 other domes were the hot baths, one of which had cocks of cold Water turning into it to temper it to what degree of warmth the bathers have a mind to.

Another favorite gathering place in the Ottoman Empire was the coffeehouse, where groups of 20 or 30 people would gather for coffee and conversation. In 1698, Antoine Galland, a French scholar of Arabic, described the coffeehouse scene in his popular book on coffee: "When conversation lagged, someone read from a book or, as many poets frequented coffee houses, someone recited his newest poem while others praised or criticized it in lively terms."

Coffeehouses moved to the West in the form of the café. They became so popular that by 1700 there were 3,000 cafés in London alone. People would come and sit, sip coffee or tea, and enjoy the company of others who had come to do the same thing. They could discuss the latest book, read the newspaper provided by the café, or discuss current events. One only has to walk the streets of Paris today to see how the café took root in Western culture.

In fact, anything Turkish became fashionable in Europe. The traders of the Levant Company kept busy shuttling coffee, carpets, and long-haired cats. Travel narratives sparked interest in coffeehouses and marching bands. Soon the most stylish were serving croissants wearing turbans, and even reading plays that dramatically revealed the Turks' opulence and wealth, acquired through greed and corruption.

Lady Mary Wortley Montagu was delighted when her husband was appointed ambassador to Adrianople, the governmental center of the Ottoman Empire. The journey to Adrianople was long and dangerous, a true adventure in those days. In addition the Montagus traveled through the dead of winter, which made it all the more challenging. Lady Mary loved every mile. She wrote long letters to her friends back in England, her humor shining through her

London coffeehouses of the early 18th century were modeled on ones that English travelers visited in the Ottoman Empire. The idea of the café as a place to gather to discuss the news of the day, socialize, and drink coffee or tea caught on all over Europe.

"All the cafés of Damascus are beautiful—lots of fountains, nearby rivers, tree-shaded spots, roses and other flowers; a cool, refreshing, and pleasant spot."

—Jean de Thévenot, French traveler, on the coffeehouses of Damascus in the Ottoman Empire, 1727

every observation. Along the way, she read voraciously about the Ottoman Empire—everything she could get her hands on—the Quran, Turkish poetry, and a best-selling collection of exciting tales called *The Thousand and One Nights*, a book that was wildly popular with the aristocratic ladies in Europe. The book overflowed with harrowing plots, exotic settings, and unfamiliar characters. Lady Mary, along with all the other readers of *The Thousand and One Nights*, was left craving more.

For Lady Mary, living in an exotic place was a fabulous opportunity. She wasn't about to sit inside the embassy like other European wives. She learned the Turkish language, dressed in traditional Turkish clothing—head covering and all—and set out to explore this strange new place. Lady Mary was fascinated by the architecture, particularly admiring the beauty of the mosques. She spoke with Turkish women and soon admired them as well.

Her experiences were much different than what she had read about back in England and during her journey. She hoped to correct all those misconceptions and particularly hoped to portray the lives of women properly. All the travel writers before her had been men, and their writings on women had been all guesswork, since they were not allowed to enter women's living quarters. She wrote in a letter home, "Now I am a little acquainted with their ways, I cannot forbear admiring either the exemplary discretion or extreme Stupidity of all the writers that have given accounts of 'em."

Local women warmly welcomed Lady Mary even though she must have looked quite foreign to them, a courtesy she

The Ottoman Method in Action

" **LADY MARY WORTLEY MONTAGU,
LETTER TO SARAH CHISWELL, APRIL 1, 1717**

*As wife of the British ambassador, Lady Mary Wortley Montagu lived in the
Ottoman Empire in the early 18th century. A few years before moving to
Istanbul, Lady Mary had suffered from smallpox, a dread disease that produced sores all over the body, and left some victims blind. Lady Mary had permanent scars from her bout with smallpox; her brother had died of the disease.
Therefore, when she learned of the Ottoman method for inoculating against
smallpox, she had her son inoculated. In April 1718 she sent her sister the following account of the procedure. Four years later, after she had returned to
England, she tried to convince others of its benefits. There was opposition
to the inoculation method, but later, once it was proven safe, many English
people did get inoculated. However, Mary Montagu never got the credit she
deserved for saving so many lives by pushing the medical community to take
a closer look at inoculation.*

I am going to tell you a thing that will make you wish yourself here. The
small-pox, so fatal and so general amongst us, is here entirely harmless
by the invention of ingrafting, which is the term they give it. There is a
set of old women who make it their business to perform the operation
every autumn, in the month of September, when the great heat is abat-
ed. People send to one another to know if any of their family has a mind
to have the small-pox; they make parties for this purpose, and when they
are met (commonly fifteen together) the old woman comes with a nut-
shell full of the matter of the best sort of small-pox, asks what vein you
please to have opened. She immediately rips open that you offer to her
with a large needle (which gives you no more pain that a common
scratch), and puts into the vein as much matter as can lie upon the head
of her needle, and after that binds up the little wound with a hollow bit
of shell; and in this manner opens four or five veins. . . . The children or
young patients play together all the rest of the day, and are in perfect
health to the eighth [day]. Then the fever begins to seize them, and they
keep their beds two days, very seldom three. They have rarely above
twenty or thirty [pock marks] in their faces, which never mark; and in
eight days time they are as well as before their illness.

With her letters and other writings, Lady Mary Wortley Montagu left a vivid record of a European's view of Ottoman society at the height of the empire. "'Tis true their Magnificence is of a different taste from ours, and perhaps better... I am almost of opinion they have a right notion of life; they consume it in music, gardens, wine, and delicate eating, while we are fomenting our brains with some scheme of politics or studying some science to which we can never attain."

doubted European women would have extended if the situation were reversed. "I was in my travelling Habit, which is a rideing dress, and certainly appear'd very extrordinary to them," she wrote to a friend, "yet there was not one of 'em that shew'd the least surprise or impertinent Curiosity, but receiv'd me with all the obliging civility possible. I know no European Court where the Ladys would have behav'd them selves in so polite a manner to a stranger."

Lady Mary was particularly impatient with friends in England who expected the Ottomans to be somehow circuslike freaks instead of ordinary people. Beneath the differences in clothing and customs, she found they were no different than the Europeans in their hopes and dreams. But her friends at home wanted tall tales for their entertainment. After writing a testy response to one friend, Lady Mary had regrets and wrote to her sister:

I have writ a letter to Lady—that I believe she won't like, and upon cooler refflexion, I think I had done better to leave it alone, but I was downright peevish at all her Questions and her ridiculous imagination that I have certainly seen an abundance of wonders that I keep to my self out of sheer malice. She is angry that I won't lie like other travelers. I verily believe she expects I should tell her of the Anthropophagi [cannibals] [and] men whose heads grow below their shoulders.

Many of Lady Mary's letters were published in England. It was not long before she found herself the most celebrated writer on the Ottoman Empire in the 18th century. In fact, she was probably the most renowned female travel writer anywhere. During her travels through the empire, Mary Montagu discovered that the Ottomans had found a treatment that prevented smallpox. She learned that doctors deliberately infected their patients with a mild form of the disease. By doing this, their patients developed an immunity to smallpox that protected them from its more serious effects. "There is no example of any one that has died in it," she reported, "and you may believe I am well satisfied of the safety of this experiment, since I intend to try it on my dear little son."

Although the Europeans found much to admire in Ottoman culture, the Ottomans were much more selective in what they took from Europe. European foods did not appeal to Turkish palates, but earlier in the 16th century they had borrowed cannons as well as sailing ships. And by the early 17th century Ottoman officials demanded that ambassadors from Europe bring them gifts of mechanical clocks and watches. The Turks allowed Western printing presses to operate for a short while in the 18th century and even allowed printing in Turkish. A Hungarian convert to Islam, Ibrahim Muteferrika, built and operated a Turkish press in Istanbul in the early 18th century. The scribes, people who copied written works by hand, opposed Muteferrika's press because they worried they would lose their jobs (and their high standing in the empire). So a compromise was struck. Muteferrika could print books about history, geography, languages, mathematics, and the sciences, as long as he left the making of books on religious subjects to the scribes.

Another of the few Western products the Ottomans did find useful was guns. This isolation from other people and their ideas and customs would contribute mightily to the collapse of the Ottoman Empire. But despite troubles from isolation, and the expense of armies and navies to maintain control of their vast territories, the Ottomans managed to survive through reforms and revivals until World War I. It was the longest functioning empire in the history of the world—and that in itself is pretty magnificent.

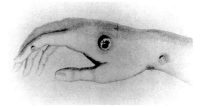

An illustration from a late–18th century medical book shows the sorts of ugly open sores caused by smallpox. Lady Mary Wortley Montagu observed the inoculation of people in the Ottoman Empire against the deadly disease and described the procedure to friends in England.

CHAPTER 4

PEACOCKS AND THE POWER OF PACHYDERMS
THE WONDERS OF MUGHAL INDIA

Shah Jahan is seated on the Peacock Throne, which was constructed especially for him in 1635 because he decided that the traditional thrones of his family were not ornate enough. The fifth Mughal emperor to take power in India, he wanted his throne to symbolize the success of the empire.

Shah Jahan did not want the six thrones that had belonged to his ancestors. He wanted his throne to show the world just how wealthy the Mughals had become in the 100 years since they had left central Asia in the early 1500s and come to India. He, after all, was the fifth in the line of Muslim emperors known as the Mughal Dynasty. He was *Zille-I-Illahi,* or Shadow of God on Earth. This could be no ordinary throne; this throne had to be spectacular. Diamonds, rubies, emeralds, garnets, and pearls were brought from the Imperial Jewel House for the emperor's inspection. He chose gems of unimaginable size—a 186-carat diamond, a 283-carat ruby—more than 100 pounds of gems in all. The gems that Shah Jahan approved of were passed along to the royal goldsmith along with more than 500 pounds of pure gold. The throne's canopy, lined with rubies, soared 15 feet high and was held aloft by emerald columns. And over the head of the emperor were solid gold peacocks, their tails brilliant with blue sapphires. This was a throne that spoke of wealth and power. On March 12, 1635, Shah Jahan, the emperor of Mughal India, climbed the three jewel-encrusted steps for the first time and sat on the Peacock Throne.

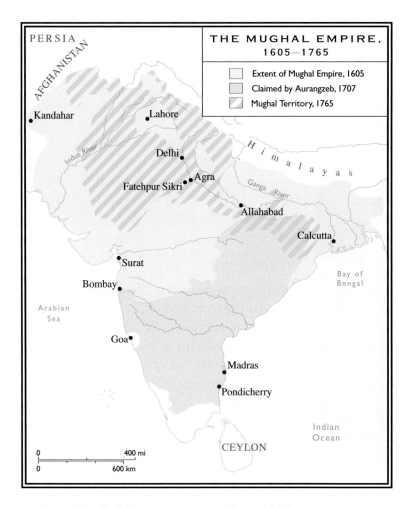

The Mughal Dynasty was a line of Muslim emperors who ruled India from 1526 to 1858. The Mughals were descendants of Turkish tribes and for several centuries had tried to move south into India. Finally, in 1523, the tribal leader called Babur (not to be confused with Babar) succeeded in this goal.

Once in power in India, the many Mughal rulers hoped to spread their Muslim faith. The largest religious group in India was the Hindus. Unlike the Muslims, who believed in just one god, Hindus believed in many gods. The Hindus also believed that people were born into a group, or caste. There were castes of low social standing and castes of high social standing and everything in between, like rungs on a

This grain seller in India was a member of a certain caste, or social group. Hindus believed that those born into a specific caste were limited to whatever trade, profession, or social standing was associated with that caste. That meant that the sons and daughters of grain sellers should marry only people of the grain seller's caste.

ladder. Each caste was associated with an occupation passed down by birth. If a father was in the priestly caste, then all his children—both boys and girls—would also be in the priestly caste. If a father were a leather craftsman, then his children would be leather craftsmen. Although the Hindus performed ceremonies that the Muslims considered offensive, such as burning incense in front of statues of spiritual beings, they were tolerated by the early Mughal rulers.

DISOBEDIENT SON

Babur's great-grandson Jahangir was a rebellious young man. In 1600, after completing a military assignment, he defied his father, Emperor Akbar the Great, by attempting to take over the Indian capital city of Agra. He appointed his own officials to run the government. He had coins made with his own name on them instead of his father's. And he told prayer leaders in local mosques to recite his name instead of his father's in the Friday prayers. Akbar was not going to stand for such disobedience. He sent threatening letters to his son telling him to stop it at once and come home. When Jahangir ignored his father's orders, Akbar knew it was time to call in the elephants.

Akbar summoned his administrators and told them to prepare his traveling army for an expedition to Agra to put an end to his son's defiance. Moving the army was no small task. Mughal mobile armies were enormous, so moving them was like moving a city. One tent took 1,000 men a whole week to put up even with elephants to do the heavy lifting. (Mughal rulers loved their elephants greatly. Some had more than 30,000 of them. And each elephant was assigned at least five stable boys to take care of it.) The army moved with as many as 300,000 men, 50,000 horses and oxen (in addition to the elephants), and all their tents, food,

The Floating "Capital" City of the Mughal Emperor

" **PETER MUNDY, TRAVELS IN EUROPE AND ASIA, 1632**

Peter Mundy was a widely traveled Englishman who worked for the British East India Company. He was in India in June 1632 and was fortunate enough to witness the extraordinary, circuslike, mobile Mughal army. In an account of his journeys Mundy describes all the possessions and types of transportation used by Mughals in their moveable life.

Myself, with Sunderdas went towards [Dahre-ka Bagh, or Dahra Garden] to see the King comeinge thither. By the way before wee could gett forth of the Cittie, wee were stopped and hindred by a great number of Eliphants, Cammells, Carts and Coaches laden with lumberment which came from the lasbkar or Campe, also many Coaches, Palanqueeenes [beds or stretchers carried on the shoulders of men] and doolees [portable, covered chairs carried by two people] with woemen. . . . Att length wee were informed whereabout the king, was himself; for all the face of the earth soe farr as wee could see was covered with people, troops, horses, Eliphants, etts [etc.], with innumerable flaggs small and great which made a most gallant show; for it is the Custome of every per-ticular great man to goe with a great many of their flaggs carried before him . . . Then thousands of horsemen going breadthwise; then came about 19 or 20 great Eliphants of state with coverings and furniture; most of them Cloth of gold, the rest rich Stuffe, velvetts, &c; some of them carrying a flagg with the kings Armes, which is a Tygar couching with the Sunne rising over his backe. . . . Then came the king himself mounted on a dark gray horse. . . . A litle distance behinde rode his eld-est sonne Daroo Shuchir [Dara-Shikoh] all alone, All the rest of the Amrawes [umaras] or Lords on foote, before and behind, and on each side of him. . . . All this moveinge in one, on soe many huge Eliphants seemed like a fleete of shipps with flagg and streamers. . . . Soe that all theis together made a most majesticall, warlike and delightful sight.

and baggage. The fact that many of the cannons they hauled along did not work is a clue that the army may have been more for a show of force than actual force. That show of force was why war elephants were so popular. What could be more intimidating than a charging elephant?

Akbar and Jahangir continued to fight each other for the next four years. Their troubles continued until Jahangir's mother could not stand it any longer. She pleaded with Jahangir to stop rebelling and make peace with his father. In a temper, Jahangir took off to the city of Allahabad. He drank too much wine and lost himself to opium addiction. When he returned home in 1604, his father confined him to his rooms for several days to sober him up.

Although Emperor Akbar had serious doubts about his son's ability to rule an empire, in the end he gave in. Akbar formally placed the royal turban on his son's head. He also presented him with his grandfather's sword, symbolically passing the power from father to son. Jahangir became emperor in 1605. Akbar died a few months later.

When Jahangir took the throne, the Mughal Empire extended from the northern border of Afghanistan southward about two thirds down the Indian peninsula. It was among the richest empires in the world. It had agricultural riches, wealth from the weaving of cottons and silks, which the Mughals sold all across Asia, and a steady supply of precious gems.

When the ships of the British East India Trading Company first arrived in the early 17th century, they came with their cargo holds full of woolen cloth, hoping to sell it in India as they did in Europe. But no one in India was interested. Indian weavers had been organized by Akbar, who like all Mughals loved color. His master dyers produced

Emperor Akbar the Great (left, holding a falcon) and his rebellious son Jahangir were often at odds. Akbar finally handed over the throne to Jahangir in 1605, even though he had serious doubts about whether Jahangir would be a good ruler.

This Indian cotton fabric from the late 18th century is painted and printed with the detailed, vividly colored designs that Europeans found appealing. The cloth became so popular in England that merchants there tried to outlaw the importation of Indian cloth because it was less expensive than their own and threatened their businesses.

dazzling colors. His master weavers produced complicated designs featuring flowers such as the lotus and birds such as the peacock. Some designs also featured the *boteh*, an Indian symbol of fertility. Europeans had never seen lightweight washable fabric before. The British East India Company returned to England with its cargo holds full of this cotton cloth. Enchanted by the *boteh*, the English renamed the design "paisley" and took it as their own.

Cottons became so popular by the end of the 17th century that weavers and linen merchants in England tried to outlaw importing the cloth. Cloth was one of the largest industries in England at that time, second only to agriculture, and fine Indian cottons and silks were cutting into sales of English fabrics. Despite spies sent by British weavers to learn Indian weaving techniques, it wasn't until the mid-18th century that British weavers could even come close to the quality of Indian goods. In England Indian

"*F*or forty days and forty nights I caused the... great imperial state drum to strike up, without ceasing, the strains of joy and triumph; and around my throne, the ground was spread by my directions with the most costly brocades and gold embroidered carpets."

—Jahangir on his coronation in 1605, from his memoirs

Elephants were an important part of Mughal India—they helped move armies and even assisted in the execution of prisoners by trampling them to death. Although Emperor Jahangir could be gentle and fair, he also had a cruel side that enjoyed the spectacle of "death by elephant."

prints were outlawed. A person owning them could be arrested. The British East India Company traders found other eager buyers outside England and smuggled them into the country. As a result, Indian weavers and weavers prospered and the Mughal treasury grew.

A member of the British East India Company declared that Jahangir was "the greatest emperor of the East for wealth, land, and forces of men, as also horses, elephants, camels, and dromedaries." As a leader and a man, Jahangir had two faces. Thomas Roe, the chaplain to the English ambassador, reported that "sometimes he was barbarously cruel and at other times, he would seem to be exceedingly fair and gentle."

His cruel side found expression in his fascination with watching criminals crushed by elephants, a form of execution at the time. He condemned many prisoners to death by elephant just for his own entertainment. And yet his gentle side loved watching nature and wild animals. He also wrote poetry and enjoyed music. Even though most Mughal emperors spent a great deal of time in battle fighting warlords who refused to pay taxes, Jahangir did little of that. He much preferred to appreciate a painting of an elephant.

Although he already had 19 wives, in 1611 Jahangir married a beautiful, intelligent Persian woman named Nur Jahan. She was the daughter of a very important court official, and her former husband had been a soldier who died in battle. Although she was only in her 30s, once Nur Jahan became Jahangir's wife, she quickly took control of a great many court functions. She personally rewarded and promoted deserving soldiers and minted coins with her own name on them. She began to make government appointments, to collect taxes from merchants, and to construct large buildings. This was very unusual for a woman in Mughal India. But Jahangir's weakness for wine may have made him a weak leader, and Nur Jahan possessed exceptional abilities. Alexander Dow, an official who served in the British East India Company, noted that "in a government in which women are thought incapable of bearing any part...[she] stood forth in public; she broke through all restraint and custom, and acquired power."

The empress supported artists, poets, and musicians. The artists produced very detailed miniature paintings in the Mughal style; done in water-based paints, they depicted palace life and nature scenes. Nur Jahan laid out many formal gardens and was the first woman in Mughal India to commission and fully carry out the construction of a monumental building—namely, the tomb for her father.

The Mughal Empire, like most empires, was based on the collection of a variety of taxes, especially taxes on farmland. India was an agriculturally rich land whose peasants grew many different crops. Farmers grew several varieties of wheat and grain, along with spices, especially pepper, which was highly prized by Europeans. In addition, a thriving textile industry produced both cotton and silk fabrics. With the arrival of the Portuguese, Dutch, and English traders, the demand for Indian goods rose.

The British East India Company, which had been founded in 1600, first established an outpost in India in 1616. The very next year Emperor Jahangir welcomed the British. His letter to the king of England makes it sound as if his eagerness for the British to come to India stemmed from greed: "I desire your Majesty to command your merchants to bring in their ships of all sorts of rarities and rich goods fit for my palace."

The British were eager as well. They wanted to buy cotton, silk, indigo, and tea from the Indian merchants. So they established large buildings called "factories" throughout

The Honourable East India Company has a house [in Agra], a quiet place in the heart of the city where we live according to the custom of the country. The rooms...are covered with carpets with great round high cushions to lean on: we sit on the ground at our meat or discourse.

—Peter Mundy, *First Voyage to India,* 1628–1634

An English official, with an Indian boy servant at his side, looks out over the land. After the British East India Company opened India to trade, Britain made it a colony ruled by such officials.

India. These buildings were not the type of factories that we know today, but places where the representatives of the British East India Company, the "factors," could do business. They used the buildings to store large quantities of items that they had bought from Indian peasants and middlemen. Then they shipped it all back to England, or in some cases to China and to America. Some of all that gold and silver coming in from the New World went toward buying Indian goods. Mughal India was benefiting significantly from the expanding European sea trade.

AN ELEPHANT NEVER FORGETS

Much of the Mughals' profit from selling goods went into building spectacular buildings and spacious gardens. The most spectacular of these buildings was the Taj Mahal. It was built by Jahangir's son Shah Jahan—the very same Shah Jahan who built the Peacock Throne. Shah Jahan ruled with a steadier hand than his father, who was prone to mood swings and drunkenness. He was also a better military officer and state manager than his father. The wealth of the empire increased dramatically under his guidance, along with a new flowering of the arts and architecture.

Using her power as empress and stepmother of Shah Jahan, Nur Jahan arranged the marriage of her niece, Mumtaz Mahal, to her stepson. Shah Jahan fell deeply in love with Mumtaz. She was said to be a great beauty and traveled frequently with the emperor. But she died in her late 30s, after giving birth to her 14th child. The emperor was so grief-stricken that he went into seclusion for two years. It is said that he was so sad that his hair and beard turned snow white almost immediately after her death. As Mumtaz lay dying, Shah Jahan made several promises to her. One that he kept was building the Taj Mahal, a tribute to his eternal love. The white marble building materials were brought in from all over India and central Asia by 1,000 elephants. The Taj Mahal was a stunning tomb, surrounded by gardens and a reflecting pool, dedicated to the memory of his young wife. It took 26 years to build—and despite its magnificence, it cost only half as much as the Peacock Throne.

While Shah Jahan mourned his lost love, one of his four sons was busy preparing to take the throne by force. His name was Aurangzeb. As a young boy, Aurangzeb showed

The Dutch East India Company established this "factory" in Bengal. This was not a factory as we think of one, but a place where merchants bought and sold goods. Surrounded by a wall, the factory included centrally located offices for Dutch officials, as well as open courtyards and neatly planted gardens. In the background was an encampment of Indians, probably soldiers, who used elephants and horses for transportation and to haul heavy loads.

A modern view of the marble Taj Mahal shows the mausoleum's almost mystical beauty. Construction of the Taj Mahal, built in memory of Mumtaz Mahal by her husband, Emperor Shah Jahan, began in 1632, about a year after her death, and took nearly 27 years to complete.

no fear. When he was 17, an elephant broke free and charged the building where he and his father sat. Aurangzeb jumped up and drew his sword, ready to fight the enraged beast single-handedly. Fortunately—we will never know for whom, Aurangzeb or the elephant—the trainer got the elephant back under control.

Battle and war were as much a part of Mughal rulers as the air they breathed. Royal princes began their military training early. Empires expanded on the battlefield. The victors of these wars acquired riches. If you wanted wealth, power, or land, you fought. Brotherly love meant nothing. These were not your average sibling rivalries—these were battles to the death. Aurangzeb fought his brothers until they were killed or subdued. Aurangzeb also took his father, Shah Jahan, prisoner. From his prison cell in the Great Red Fort, the emperor could see with the aid of a mirror the Taj Mahal where his true love was laid to rest. During the years he was imprisoned he must have spent his days and nights watching the white marble with its inlaid jewels change color with the light. In the early morning the Taj Mahal turns pink from the sunrise, by noon it is pure white, and in the moonlight a pale gold. Shah Jahan waited to join Mumtaz—until he died in 1666.

Aurangzeb, the last of the great Mughal emperors, ruled for half a century, from 1658 to 1707. He changed the tone of the Mughal Empire. Aurangzeb was an extremely devout Muslim who spent the first seven years of his reign memorizing the Quran. Aurangzeb's strong commitment to Islam drove him to intolerance. He forbade the public performance of Hindu rituals. He forbade the public display of Hindu religious offerings. He discontinued the Mughal tradition of building great monuments and closed the artists' shops that had produced outstanding Mughal art. He assigned special police to enforce rules of trade and public conduct in the markets.

In addition, Aurangzeb required women to wear headscarves in public, and he tried to stop the sale of alcohol. All non-Muslims had to pay a tax. In India at that time Muslims were in the minority, and the non-Muslims resented Aurangzeb for forcing Islamic law and custom on them. In particular, they hated the tax. When the Hindus of India revolted, Aurangzeb turned the elephants on them. But the Hindus did not give up. Each time the emperor tried to attend his mosque, Hindu rioters blocked his way. And each time, Aurangzeb drove his elephants over their bodies. But not even stampeding elephants stopped the Hindus' outrage.

Toward the end of Aurangzeb's rule, the network of nobles, tax collectors, and court officials began to fall apart. The landholders who were supposed to collect revenue and send it to the royal treasury did not. In fact, they began to keep their armies under their own control instead of following the emperor's orders. A royal inspector and accountant during the reign of Aurangzeb remarked on how the emperor neglected his people: "The Emperor, seized with a passion for capturing forts, has given up attending to the happiness of the subjects."

An ivory shrine from the late 17th or early 18th century depicts various Hindu gods and goddesses, including Vishnu, the god of civilized society, who reclines on a bed of snakes. At this time Hindus were not allowed to worship openly, as they had been throughout the time of the Mughals in India. Therefore, a shrine like this might not have been allowed in a public place.

Jai Singh's observatory in New Delhi consists of numerous structures, all of which are actually instruments that measure astronomical phenomena such as the positions of planets. The towerlike structure in the center is the Samrat Yantra, or "supreme instrument," which acts as a giant sundial.

After Aurangzeb's death, there was a small cultural renaissance in parts of India. One governor, Jai Singh, became noted for his architectural designs and city planning. Jai Singh was also a mathematician and astronomer who built several observatories. The first was built in Delhi in 1728. These observatories were not based on the new European models and instruments, but those of the 15th-century mathematician and astronomer Ulugh Beg.

Ulugh Beg was one of the last great astronomers and mathematicians in the Islamic tradition. His important astronomical tables contained hundreds of observations of the stars, which showed their positions in the sky in different seasons and times of night. They were shared all over the Muslim world, including India. Jai Singh studied this work and modeled his observatory after that of Ulugh Beg. Jai Singh laid out the construction plans for four other observatories and gave instructions for sighting and measuring the locations of stars and planets before he died in 1743.

Despite this short renaissance, the Mughal Dynasty was finished. The Mughal rulers were too weak to hold the empire together after Aurangzeb died. Local princes asserted their power to create their own armies and to withhold taxes from the imperial treasury. At the same time, British officials sent out by the British East India Company were gaining more and more administrative control over Indian territories and affairs. Meanwhile, Europeans were bringing back plants and animals to expand their knowledge. With them, they built botanical gardens, circuses, and zoos. Eventually the Europeans even brought home elephants—magnificent living examples of the glory days of the Mughal Empire.

CHAPTER 5

MISSIONARIES, MAPS, AND MAGISTRATES WITH PINK PARASOLS
CHINA ENCOUNTERS MODERN SCIENCE

It is hard to imagine that just 500 years ago, the location of a place as large as China was a mystery to most Europeans. The Ming Empire of China was a vast, sprawling, centrally organized kingdom, and yet Westerners knew next to nothing about it. Yes, the Venetian explorer Marco Polo had traveled to a place he called Cathay in the late 13th century, but was that China? On the other hand, the Chinese did not know much about the Europeans either. They had no idea how their own country looked on a world map. Where was China located in relation to Europe and the landmass that formed Asia? No one—neither European nor Chinese—knew for sure. This was the puzzle Father Matteo Ricci tackled when he arrived in China in 1582. Ricci was one of those fearless Jesuit missionaries who set off into the unknown in the late 16th century to find and convert more souls to Christianity.

Matteo Ricci was born in Italy in 1552. Ricci must have had deep religious beliefs, because he entered a Jesuit school even though his father was so opposed to religion that he would not allow anyone to discuss it in their home. In school Ricci learned to speak and read Latin, and he discovered he was good at learning languages in general. He had a gift for memorization. He studied Greek before he began to study law. His university studies also included physics, astronomy, mathematics, logic, and philosophy.

When Ricci finished his religious training, he requested that the Jesuits send him to China as a missionary. But he could not be honest with the Chinese government about why

"In order that the appearance of a new religion might not arouse suspicion among the Chinese people, the Fathers did not speak only about religious matters when they began to appear in public. ... They did, however, endeavor to teach ... in a more direct way, namely, by virtue of their example and by the sanctity of their lives."

—Matteo Ricci, *Journals*, 1583–1610

Tome III.page 78.

Matteo Ricci was both a priest and a scientist. He went to China with the intention of converting the people to Christianity, but his greatest achievement was promoting the latest advances in Western science, especially astronomy, to the skeptical Chinese. The map in Ricci's hand reflects the fact that he produced for the Chinese the first world map that included Europe, Africa, and parts of the New World previously not represented on Chinese maps.

he wanted to come. If he had told the Chinese that he hoped to spread a new religion, they would not have let him into the country. The Chinese did not believe that a foreigner could possibly have anything of value to teach them. The missionaries were told that, when questioned about their motives, they should answer that they were priests who were moving to China because of the Chinese government's wonderful reputation throughout the world.

Even this flattery might not be enough to get permission from the emperor or his officials to enter China. The Chinese government kept a very careful watch over foreigners. "The Chinese never allow foreigners to settle down in their country," wrote the French Jesuit Louis Le Comte in the mid-18th century. At first Ricci had difficulty being accepted by the Chinese, who distrusted foreigners. Suspicious landlords drove Ricci out of their houses time after time until Ricci came up with an ingenious plan: He rented houses that local residents believed to be haunted and no one else wanted to rent as a result. The landlords left him alone after that.

Ricci realized that he would be more successful converting the Chinese if he could speak to them in their own language. Therefore, the first thing he did when he arrived in China was learn Chinese. Chinese is a complicated language, with a huge number of words and characters, so memorization is extremely important in learning it. Ricci had several methods for memorizing long lists of words. He also invented a system that matched Chinese characters, which are graphic symbols, with the corresponding words in Latin.

In fact, Ricci was the first to work out such a system comparing Chinese characters and Latin words. Missionaries before him did not have his natural talent with languages

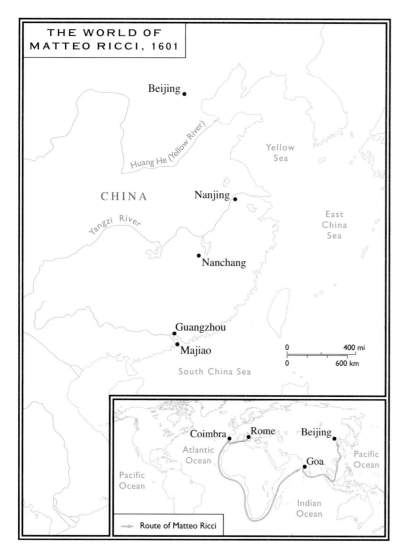

THE WORLD OF
MATTEO RICCI, 1601

Beijing

Huang He (Yellow River)

Yellow
Sea

CHINA

Nanjing

East
China
Sea

Yangzi River

Nanchang

Guangzhou

Majiao

South China Sea

0   400 mi
0   600 km

Coimbra   Rome   Beijing

Atlantic
Ocean

Pacific
Ocean

Pacific
Ocean

Goa

Indian
Ocean

➤ Route of Matteo Ricci

and had struggled, never becoming fluent. Ricci explained in a letter home what made Chinese so difficult to learn: "There are many words that can signify more than a thousand things, and at times the only difference between one word and another is the way you pitch them high or low in four different tones."

Ricci threw himself wholeheartedly into his studies. He became a true master of the Chinese language. But he didn't stop there. He studied Chinese philosophy, law, and science. He even dressed like the mandarins, the Chinese scholars

> "*I* am of the opinion that the Chinese possess the ingenuous trait of preferring that which comes from without to that which they possess themselves, once they realize the superior quality of the foreign product. Their pride, it would seem, arises from an ignorance of the existence of higher things and from the fact that they find themselves far superior to the barbarous nations by which they are surrounded."
>
> —Matteo Ricci, *Journals*, 1583–1610.

who passed many exams to achieve their high official status. Soon Chinese people were calling him "the Wise Man from the West."

KNOWLEDGE IS POWER

Now Ricci was ready to begin his true mission—spreading the word of Christianity. But how? The Chinese were very proud of their culture. They believed the whole world, except for China, was populated by barbarians. Ricci would have to appeal to their curiosity. Perhaps if he were able to tickle that curiosity, he could teach them about his religion.

Ricci hung a picture of the Virgin Mary holding the baby Jesus in the room where visitors would see it. When they asked about the picture, Ricci answered in a way that introduced them to Christianity. Ricci also scattered about his home astronomical instruments, clocks, prisms (glass objects that fractured light into colors), papers covered with mathematical scribblings, and maps—lots of maps. The Chinese at first were shocked. Why was this man not an ignorant barbarian? He should be, after all—he was not Chinese. But their curiosity got the better of them, and soon Ricci's home overflowed with visitors. His mini-museum attracted the educated, even the most respected scholars—the mandarins.

Through Ricci's discussions with the scholars, he discovered gaps between European knowledge and Chinese knowledge. In

An astrolabe was one of the scientific instruments that Matteo Ricci kept in his home in China to pique his Chinese visitors' interest in Western science. An astrolabe was used to observe and calculate the position of celestial bodies, such as planets.

one of his letters he wrote, "Because of my world-map, my clocks...and other things I do and teach, I have gained the reputation of being the greatest mathematician in the world. I am able...to predict the eclipses more accurately than they do."

Ricci hoped that he could use this impression that he was "the greatest mathematician" in the world to his advantage in his missionary work. If Western science could be linked to Christianity, then, Ricci thought, this might be a way to get the Chinese to convert to Christianity.

Ricci's reputation for studying all things Chinese—not to mention having all those interesting gadgets—attracted plenty of Chinese scholars. Ricci was interested in what their schooling was like compared to his own. A well-educated Chinese scholar was trained to understand the ancient writings and sayings of the Chinese philosopher Confucius. These writings from the 6th century BCE are a collection of moral and ethical teachings, poetry, historical accounts, and sacred texts. Not all of them were written by Confucius, but sayings like this one have been attributed to him and preserved in books called the *Analects:* "The superior man understands righteousness; the inferior man understands profit." The Chinese believed that studying and memorizing these texts was the path to scholarly enlightenment. "The Master said, 'If the people be led by laws...they will try to avoid *the punishments,* but have no sense of shame. If they be led by virtue...they will have the sense of shame, and moreover will become good.'"

Village schools were the first step on a very long educational path marked by exam after exam. Parents proudly raised flags over their homes to announce when a son passed another important exam. Private tutoring was necessary to help students master written Chinese and the Confucian classics. A promising student might get to learn from a scholar who had already passed the exams. Scholars who won the highest academic honors in examinations were appointed to be magistrates, or town officials. The magistrates were

A 17th-century artist portrayed the philosopher Confucius, who lived in the 6th century BCE. Confucius is wearing the elaborate robes of a Chinese scholar while carrying scrolls of text. In the 17th century, a Chinese scholar's education required mastering the teachings of Confucius along with history and poetry.

continues on page 80

Rules to Live By

66 | **ZHU XI, ARTICLES OF INSTRUCTION, AROUND 1180**

The philosopher Zhu Xi gave China a new understanding of the ideas of the ancient wise man Confucius. Zhu Xi's works from the 12th century were taught in schools throughout China and the rest of East Asia until the 20th century to young students aspiring to become scholar-sages. His work instructed readers in how to deal with others, how to respect their parents, how to revere the emperor, and how to manage daily life. The first five lines below refer to the set of core relationships that were thought to be the most important for society.

> Affection between parent and child;
> Righteousness between ruler and subject;
> Differentiation between husband and wife;
> Precedence between elder and younger;
> Trust between friends.

The above are the items of the Five Teachings. When Yao [the ancient sovereign ruler] and Shun appointed Hsieh to be Minister of Education and to set forth reverently the Five Teachings, it was precisely these teachings. Students should study these and nothing more. In studying, there is a proper sequence, which likewise involves five items, listed separately below:

> Study extensively, inquire carefully, ponder
> thoroughly, sift clearly, and practice earnestly.

The above is the proper sequence for studying. Studying, inquiring, pondering, and sifting are the means by which to probe [moral] principle. As to earnest practice, its essence is present in every step from self-cultivation on down to handling affairs and dealing with others, as follows:

> Be loyal and true to your every word, serious
> and careful in all you do.
> Curb your anger and restrain your lust; move
> toward the good and correct your errors.

The above are the essentials of self-cultivation.

> Accord with the righteous, do not seek profit; illuminate the Way, do not calculate the advantages.

The above are the essentials for handling affairs.

> Do not do to others what you do not want done to you. Whenever you fail to achieve your purpose, look into yourself.

The above are the essentials for dealing with others.

In a Confucian classroom, young students are in the middle of a lesson as a teacher looks on. The student in front of the teacher's desk appears to be having a hard time, while the classmates seem amused. Perhaps this student was having difficulty with the central message of Zhu Xi's reinterpretation of Confucius, that one must "grasp the principles of things."

continued from page 77

celebrities. Crowds would part when people heard them coming. The magistrates came in all levels of importance; the lower levels rode horses, while the more important officials were carried in chairs on their servants' shoulders. Ricci wrote that the Chinese could tell their magistrates apart by the color of the parasols they carried to protect themselves from the sun.

The carefully ordered Chinese educational system was something that Europeans admired. But despite the Chinese openness to education, it was an education focused on the classics, not on scientific innovation or making scientific discoveries. Chinese scientists, Ricci discovered, believed that the earth was flat and square, and that the heavens were like a canopy or umbrella held overhead. Having sailed around the world to China, Ricci had no doubt that the world was round, as Western scholars believed.

Ricci displayed maps of the world in his home. At first, Chinese scholars were outraged by these maps, in particular, at how puny China looked on these descriptions of the world. Chinese maps, in contrast, showed China filling up almost the entire space, with some water on the edges dotted with a few tiny islands labeled with the names of a few places they had heard of.

The Chinese scholars argued that Ricci's maps had to be wrong. China could not be so small a part of the world.

Chinese scholars, including artists and musicians, listen to music, read scrolls, and talk in a wooded area away from the bustle of everyday life. Scholars did not always live such lives of restful meditation close to nature—they were often appointed as local magistrates or other government officials.

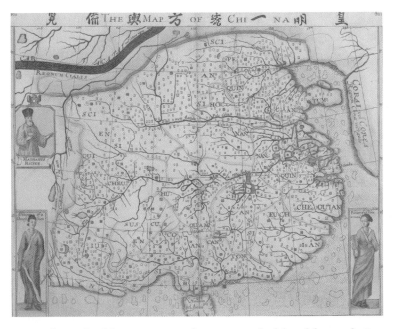

This map was made in the 1620s by an English writer who used it to illustrate a book about travels in China. It shows the Chinese provinces and major cities. The figure of Matteo Ricci that appears in the upper-left-hand corner of this map suggests that Europeans considered Ricci an important link to the distant and little-known country.

Ricci described how geographers recorded land boundaries and managed to convince the Chinese scholars to look closely at his maps. They urged Ricci to make copies of his maps and label them in Chinese. Ricci drew an even larger and more detailed map. When it was finished, the Chinese governor had copies made to give as presents to all his friends. This acceptance opened more doors for Ricci. Now more people were eager to learn about European ways from the missionaries.

Ricci discovered that the Chinese knew nothing about geometry. Without geometry it was impossible to chart the stars and accurately predict astronomical events such as eclipses accurately. And making accurate predictions was very important to the Chinese because they thought the movements of the stars and planets were connected to the good and bad behavior of the emperor. The Chinese labeled dates as either "lucky" or "unlucky" times for conducting business according to the position of the stars and planets. It would not do for the emperor or other officials to carry out duties in "unlucky" times. There was even a government ministry dedicated to the study of the stars. The office of "Rites," which ensured that all official ceremonies were

A Chinese illustration from 1580 shows an eclipse, which the Chinese interpreted as an omen of possible war and bloodshed and the overthrow of the emperor. At that time, the purpose of most Chinese astronomical study was to make calendars to determine "lucky" and "unlucky" days for conducting business and holding events such as weddings, based on the positions of the planets and other celestial bodies.

carried out properly, was also in charge of mathematics and astronomy. By using mathematics and astronomy, officials could determine the alignments of stars and planets and make calendars.

Ricci knew he would have to understand the Chinese government if he were to have any success spreading the word of Christianity. The government was a complicated spiderweb of high and low offices, each run by a highly trained literary scholar, the mandarin. This whole bustling network was controlled by the wishes and demands of the emperor himself, the spider pulling all those strings.

When Ricci arrived in Beijing in 1600, an emperor of the Ming Dynasty ruled China. Emperor Zhu Yizhun had come to power when he was nine years old, and he ruled for 48 years. He was a weak, unpredictable, and reclusive emperor notorious for neglecting his duties. He refused to meet with officials and often failed to make public appearances. He ignored his duty to appoint officials. He was so neglectful that thousands of state offices in Beijing were vacant.

With so many vacant offices, who was running the country? One exasperated official, the minister of personnel, wrote of the near collapse of the central government because the emperor would not make any new appointments. He wrote, "officials argue about the good and bad points of things... in order to influence the emperor... His disregard of them is like a paralysis for which there is no cure."

For 20 years, Ricci tried again and again to get an audience with the emperor. But the reclusive emperor denied every request—until one day Ricci received a surprise summons. The Jesuits had given the emperor a clock that had stopped ringing, and none of the emperor's scientists could fix it. Ricci was asked to come and fix the clock. But since the emperor would not allow a foreigner to see him in person, he had artists draw full-length pictures of him to be propped up in front of Ricci when he came to the palace. Ricci never did get a real audience with the emperor.

Another opportunity for the Jesuits to show the Chinese that Westerners were not barbarians happened when they made a prediction about the timing of a solar eclipse that was very different from the Chinese predictions—and turned out to be right. Even so, the emperor would not insult his mathematicians by replacing them with foreigners. The missionary astronomers had to wait two decades for another chance, until 1629, when the eclipse experiment was repeated.

On the day before the experiment, representatives of Chinese astronomical traditions and the missionaries representing the West were asked to write down their predictions of the exact time they expected the eclipse of the sun to occur. The Chinese mathematicians predicted a two-hour eclipse, starting at 10:30 in the morning and ending at 12:30. The missionaries predicted that it would begin at 11:30 in the morning and last for only two minutes. And that is exactly what happened. The emperor demanded to know why his officials failed. Was it a mathematical error? His officials knew they had not made a calculation mistake; rather, their whole system was faulty. They urged the emperor to hire the missionaries to teach them their system and fix the Chinese calendar. At the same time, they asked the emperor to launch a major translation effort so that the ideas in Western scientific books on astronomy, geometry,

"All the favors that we have obtained up to now have been given by the Emperor as payment for services rendered in the field of mathematics."

—Ferdinand Verbiest, Jesuit missionary in China from the 1660s to 1680s

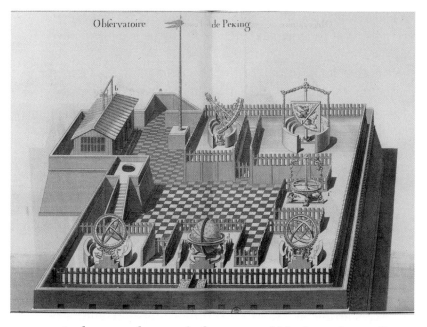

Obſervatoire   de Peking

This drawing represents the Chinese observatory in Beijing after it had been updated with European instruments under the guidance of Ferdinand Verbiest. Europeans had been trying for years to convince the emperor that their astronomical methods were more accurate than those of the Chinese. After the Europeans successfully predicted an eclipse in 1629, they won the emperor's permission to rebuild the observatory.

agriculture, and control of water could be brought to China. This time, the emperor agreed and the big project began.

Although the Jesuits never accomplished their goal of mass conversions of the Chinese to Christianity, the work of Ricci and the other Jesuit missionaries bridged the gap between Chinese and Western culture. Through their work, Westerners learned a lot about Chinese language and lifestyles. They learned about schools available to village children, and they learned about governments run by educated officials rather than aristocrats and their relatives, as was the case in many places in the West at that time. At the same time, the translation of many European books by the Jesuits gave the Chinese new access to Western ideas about science and other subjects. By introducing Europe's sciences to China and China's ancient culture to Europe, Ricci helped to change mistrust and suspicion into respect and admiration.

MADE IN CHINA

In September 1746, the board of directors of the Verenigde Oostindische Compagnie (VOC), or the Dutch United East India Company, approved the building of six new cargo ships. The director was given the honor of naming one. The VOC's tradition was to name vessels after estates belonging to the officials naming the ship, and so the director named his ship *Geldermalsen,* after his family home. Construction began a month later. The ship was to be of impressive size—42 feet wide and 150 feet long. Nine months later the *Geldermalsen* was finished.

In August 1748, the captain ordered the crew to cast off and the *Geldermalsen* took to the seas. The crew loaded and unloaded merchandise many times. In some ports they spent months collecting merchandise to fill the cargo holds before setting sail for the next port. They had at least one run-in with pirates, but they warded off the attack and made it to the safety of a port before heading to China.

It was July 1751 when the *Geldermalsen* joined other VOC ships waiting to be loaded in Guangzhou. The *Geldermalsen's* next destination was to be the Netherlands, with a whole new crew and captain. The new captain was not at all happy with how the ship was outfitted. He requested compasses, maps, and ship parts from other VOC ships. The drinking water was moldy so he replaced it. And the food supplies were low. He asked his sister ships for enough "ordinary" (that is, non-Chinese) food for the five months it would take to get to a place on the way where they could restock their provisions. The ship was also stocked with weapons—cannons, guns, and swords—for use against pirates, and leg irons to restrain any problem seamen. The captain shared his cabin with a paying passenger—an Englishman eager to get back to Europe. The captain squeezed in with his Bible, candlestick, four pillows, and chamber pot, ready for the trip home.

"I live amongst them, I have daily dealings with them. Very often I offer them the doctrine of salvation, but...I get nowhere."

—Jesuit missionary Adam Schall on his lack of success in converting the Chinese, letter to a friend, 1651

On December 18, 1751, the captain and 111 others aboard the *Geldermalsen* left Guangzhou, hoping to arrive home in July if the winds were with them. Another 16 days out of port, the *Geldermalsen* was just above the equator. There was a calm northerly wind blowing in fair skies. At half past three in the afternoon the captain climbed up on deck and asked the boatswain for their location. After making adjustments to their course, the captain retired to his cabin. Just before dark the watchman climbed up for a lookout. There was no land in sight. As darkness set in and visibility grew dim, the boatswain prepared the anchors. While looking out he spotted white froth—breakers! He shouted to the helm to shift the sails, but it was too late. With a crack felt through every seaman's bones, the *Geldermalsen* crashed onto a reef.

In mass confusion, seamen raced around the deck trying to follow the captain's orders. The *Geldermalsen* turned sideways, groaning, as it pulled away from the reef. Just as the ship came off the reef, the wind caught a starboard sail and it ran aground again. The impact toppled the topmast and shattered the tiller. The front of the ship was split open. The sick were carried to the lifeboat, just before the *Geldermalsen* capsized. Most of the seamen couldn't swim, and even if they could, finding them in the dark would have been next to impossible. The ship and all but 32 men sank to the bottom.

The wreck of the *Geldermalsen* was found in 1986. There was not much left of it after laying on the muddy sea bottom for more than 200 years. But some things can survive years of submersion, such as gold, bronze, and porcelain. The 203 crates and packing material that held the porcelain are long gone, but the 160,000 pieces of china remain. Among the historical treasure trove were some 63,000 teacups and 20,000 coffee cups.

A shipwreck can be like a time capsule. The cargo of the *Geldermalsen* gives us a glimpse into the porcelain trade in 18th-century China. In the 18th century the VOC's trading ships numbered 200. Not all traded in porcelain, and not many carried as many pieces as the *Geldermalsen*, but still, tens of millions of pieces were exported to Europe.

The West gets the name "china" from the exquisite porcelain that originated in China. And the VOC surely changed the course of "china's" history. Before 1600 few pieces made their way to Europe, and those that did came in seamen's duffels. After 1600, though, Dutch merchants engaged in an increasingly vigorous trade. The traditional stoneware of Europe could not compare to the technically superior Chinese products. It was not long before the ceramics were being copied all over Europe. A blue and white imitation of Chinese ceramics made in a city called Delft in the Netherlands became popular.

However, Europeans preferred the real thing, and commissioned decorations such as family coats of arms and European country scenes. Others preferred designs of Chinese figures, landscapes, and architecture. The designs ended up having a European influence that made the pictures not exact replicas of the Chinese designs, but "Chinese-like." This new 17th-century style of porcelain, called chinoiserie, became very popular in the early 18th century.

An intricate German porcelain figurine dating from 1765 called "The Merchant" is a fine example of European decorative style imitating that of the Chinese. European artisans perfected this style after they became familiar with Chinese porcelain designs in the 17th century.

One particular style of chinoiserie was called Pronk Porcelain, and it came about because the VOC was facing stiff competition from other trading companies. Hoping for a chance to make huge profits by providing wealthy Europeans with high-quality Chinese porcelain, the VOC commissioned a Dutch painter named Cornelius Pronk to come up with several chinoiserie designs. The Pronk Porcelain was designed in Europe but manufactured in China.

The idea may have been a good one, but the cost to the VOC to produce the porcelain in China was so expensive they could not make a profit. Not only that, but the process of creating Pronk Porcelain, from drawing to finished product, took years. For example, Pronk's well-known 1734 drawing of ladies carrying parasols didn't arrive back in the Netherlands as porcelain until 1738. In the end the VOC cancelled all the orders. But Pronk Porcelain represented a new step in international trade. For the first time, trading companies did not just meet market demands. They invested in an artist to *establish* a demand. Even though the experiment failed, it was an important exchange of art and ideas.

The "parasol ladies" was one of the most popular porcelain designs made by Dutch painter Cornelius Pronk. Pronk porcelain was made in China in the 18th century from European designs. The parasol, a type of umbrella used as a shade from the sun, was first used in the East and introduced to Europe in the 16th century.

CHAPTER 6

THE SECRETS OF THE HEAVENS

NEW SCIENTIFIC THEORIES

Observing the stars and the heavens must go back to human beginnings. When did humans first notice patterns in the phases of the moon? When did they begin to play connect-the-dots, making pictures out of the pinpricks of light in the night sky? Ancient drawings on temple walls prove that wondering about the heavens is as old as written history itself, and no doubt older than that. When you stand with two feet firmly planted on the ground and watch the sun move across the sky, it looks as if the earth is the center of the universe. The sun and moon and all the stars seem to revolve around you while you remain rooted in the middle of it all. No wonder ancient astronomers designed a universe with the earth at its center.

A Greek astronomer named Ptolemy, who lived in Alexandria, Egypt, in the 2nd century CE, spent his life trying to pull together all the known astronomical theories and observations. However, there was one theory Ptolemy should have paid more attention to. The astronomer Aristarchus, who lived five centuries before Ptolemy, theorized that the sun was the center of the universe. He suggested that the earth rotated on its axis, the invisible line that goes through its poles, and that was why it appeared as if the sun and the stars were circling us. But Ptolemy dismissed this radical theory— it did, after all, defy common sense. How was it, he wondered, that people did not feel the earth's "violent" movement? It made much more sense that the planets, stars, and moon were guided by giant hollow balls made from some clear material (by medieval times scholars decided these balls were made of crystal), and that the balls spun with the earth in the center and the planets rolling around inside like marbles.

Ptolemy wrote 13 volumes about the movements of the sun, moon, and planets that later scholars called the *Almagest*,

"It is the duty of the astronomer to compose the history of the celestial motions through careful and skillful observation. . . . So far as hypotheses are concerned, let no one expect anything certain from astronomy, which cannot furnish it, lest he accept as the truth ideas conceived for another purpose, and depart from this study a greater fool than when he entered it."

—Nicolaus Copernicus, *On the Revolutions*, 1543

The astronomers Ptolemy, Nicolaus Copernicus, and Tycho Brahe each believed the earth held a different position in the universe. In the Ptolemaic system (top), the earth was at the center of the universe with the planets revolving around it. In Copernicus's system (center), the sun was at the center with all the other planets circling it. In Tycho Brahe's system (bottom), Mercury and Venus circled the earth, while Mars, Jupiter, and Saturn circled the sun, which in turn revolved around the earth at the center of the universe.

or "The Greatest Book." But despite his claim in the *Almagest's* introduction that "if my mind follows the winding paths of the stars, then my feet no longer rest on earth," he was unable to imagine a center of the universe other than the earth. His feet were still too firmly planted on it.

Although there were problems with Ptolemy's planetary system that had some scholars scratching their heads, no one could come up with a better model of the earth, sun, moon, and planets. And so for nearly 15 centuries, it was *the* reference for astronomers working on their own earth-based theories. When the *Almagest* was translated into Arabic, in about the 8th century CE, scholars in the Muslim world studied the translation carefully. The most expert students knew that Ptolemy's representation of the movements of the planets was incorrect. Ptolemy claimed that every planet moved at a constant speed, and that their orbits were circles. But astronomers could see that there were times when a planet sped up. And sometimes the observers found the planets in positions outside those perfectly circular orbits. Most troubling of all was the fact that the planets periodically appeared to reverse direction and move backward. Over time, it became harder to ignore that the planets were not moving according to Ptolemy's model.

By the 11th century, Arab scholars began to say openly that Ptolemy's system was defective. One vocal Muslim scholar was Ibn al-Haytham, who lived in Egypt in the 10th century. Al-Haytham carefully studied Ptolemy's *Almagest,* and he concluded that "[the] movements of the five planets is a false configuration, and that there exists for the movements of these planets a true configuration, other than that asserted by Ptolemy."

Ptolemy's model was full of flaws. Clearly a new system was needed.

STAR-CROSSED

Scholars began to rethink the world around them. One scholar in particular took on the problem with a passion. Nicolaus Copernicus was born in a small Polish town in

1473, at a time when people were curious about the world they lived in. Scholars explored everything then—mathematics, astronomy, geography, medicine, religion, art, and philosophy. But universities only offered training for three professions—theology, law, or medicine. Copernicus chose medicine. He probably chose it for practical reasons: a knowledge of medicine would be useful to the members of his local religious order in Poland, especially his uncle, who was the head of that order. But Copernicus also knew that doctors got to study the stars—and he was fascinated by the stars.

Copernicus spent every spare moment reading about the stars. He wrote pages and pages about a planetary system he believed centered around the sun. Copernicus knew that his new theory went against common sense. One only had to look up and it was *obvious* that the sun was circling the earth. He admitted, "my theory of the Earth's movement might at first seem strange."

So, fearing that people would make fun of something that went against what they could see with their own eyes, he refused again and again to publish his work. Only a few handwritten copies were passed around among his closest friends.

In the European world, Copernicus and other astronomers faced an additional problem: the fact that the Church Fathers (the Pope and all his officials) had adopted the Bible as their sacred text. According to the Bible, the earth was at the center of the universe. They quoted passages from the Holy Scriptures in support of this view. One commonly quoted passage came from the Old Testament. Joshua needed more

In 1647, the Polish astronomer Johannes Hevelius wrote a comprehensive book on the moon and its phases. The title page of the book portrayed the Arab mathematician Ibn al-Haytham (left) as a skilled user of logic and placed Galileo Galilei opposite him, with his telescope representing the powers of visual observation.

This portrait of Nicolaus Copernicus reminds the viewer that he was both a Christian and a scientist, two roles that were at odds during his lifetime. The skull reflects the church's teaching that belief in Jesus Christ triumphs over death. The compass and astronomical instrument for measuring the positions of the planets represent his scientific studies and beliefs.

> "*T*here came on the scene a certain German, one Copernicus, who made short work of all those various circles, all those solid skies, which the ancients had pictured to themselves. The former he abolished; the latter, broke in pieces. Fired with the noble zeal of a true astronomer, he took the earth and spun it very far away from the centre of the universe, where it had been installed, and in that centre he put the sun, which had a far better title to the honour."
>
> —Bernard le Bovier de Fontenelle, *L'Histoire du renouvellement de l'Académie royale des Sciences*, (History of the Renewal of the Royal Academy of Sciences), 1702

time to win a battle against his enemies, so he prayed to the Lord to stop the sun. According to Joshua 10:13, God complied: "The sun stood still and the moon halted until a nation had taken vengeance on its enemies...The sun stayed in mid heaven and made no haste to set for almost a whole day."

Who would dare to challenge the Bible? Copernicus. Despite church opposition he concluded, in a book called *On the Revolutions of the Heavenly Spheres,* that "the center of the world is around the sun." He downgraded the earth from the center of the universe to just another planet. The earth, he said, was in orbit along with the five other planets— Mercury, Venus, Mars, Jupiter and Saturn—*around the sun.*

Copernicus came up with a set of principles for a new system of astronomy that he sketched out in a short book called the *Little Commentary:*

1. There is no one center in the universe.
2. The Earth's center is not the center of the universe.
3. The center of the universe is near the sun.
4. The distance from the Earth to the sun is imperceptible compared with the distance to the stars.
5. The rotation of the Earth accounts for the apparent daily rotation of the stars.
6. The apparent annual cycle of movements of the sun is caused by the Earth revolving round it.
7. The apparent retrograde [reverse] motion of the planets is caused by the motion of the Earth from which one observes.

With this new sun-centered system, lots of puzzling astronomical observations (but not all) were cleared up. For example, the retrograde, or backward motion of the planets, could be explained by the motion of the earth. The planets weren't traveling backward at all. It was the earth moving forward. You might experience the same illusion if you were sitting in a train looking out the window at a train on the next track. Sometimes it is hard to tell which train is in motion. Are you moving forward? Or is the train next to you moving backward?

Copernicus's work, which was finally published in 1543, the year he died, clashed with the strongly held earth-centered view of the Church Fathers. In 1616 the Catholic Church put Copernicus's work on its banned books list, the *Index of Prohibited Books*, which Catholics were not allowed to read. The Protestants did not approve of Copernicus either. One Protestant leader, Martin Luther, called Copernicus an "upstart astrologer... This fool wishes to reverse the entire science of astronomy. But Sacred Scripture tells us that Joshua commanded the Sun to stand still, and not the Earth."

Before the banning, in the first decade of the 17th century, a young professor of mathematics named Galileo Galilei came across the Copernican system. He accepted it wholeheartedly, even though he knew that not all its claims could be proved. He also embraced an idea that suggested that the natural world could be studied and understood as one might read a book—the book of nature. He borrowed this idea from the scholars of the Middle Ages, who believed that the hidden things of nature could be figured out and understood "like reading a book." As Galileo put it, natural science "is written in this grand book.... It is written

The Catholic Church in Galileo's time maintained a list of books that Catholics were forbidden to read unless they were "corrected," which meant blacking out any statements that went against the teachings of the Church. Galileo's books were placed on this list and remained there for more than 200 years.

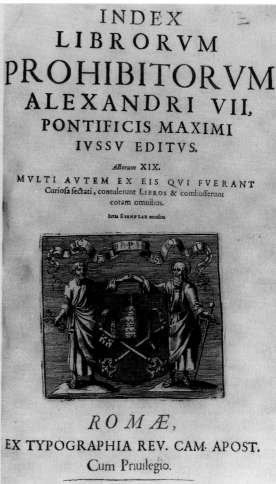

In 1610, Galileo published a book called The Starry Messenger, *in which he reported his telescopic observations of the moon. He included these drawings of the appearance of the moon in its different phases to show that the moon is "not smooth, uniform, or precisely spherical, but is uneven, rough, and full of cavities... not unlike the face of the earth."*

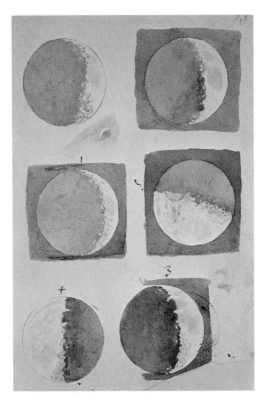

in the language of mathematics, and its characters are triangles, circles, and other geometric figures without which it is humanly impossible to understand a word of it."

For Galileo, knowledge could exist independent of the Scriptures. The debate then centered on the question, should we believe what Holy Scripture says about the natural world, or should we believe the reasoned conclusions stemming from observation? In 1615, Prince Cesi, a friend of Galileo, warned him that church officials were not happy with his ideas at all. The prince reported that Cardinal Bellarmine "has told me that he regards it as heretical and that without doubt [the belief in] the earth's motion is against Scripture." It wasn't long before Galileo was summoned before the cardinal, who ordered Galileo "to abandon completely... the opinion that the sun stands still at the center of the world and the earth moves... and not to hold, teach or defend it in any way whatever."

Despite the constant pressure, Galileo continued to write in defense of a sun-centered system. Galileo rejected the church's literal interpretation of the Bible. Instead of believing that the Bible was a guide for astronomers, he said, "the intention of the Holy Spirit is to teach us how one goes to heaven and not how heaven goes." His book *Dialogue of Two World Systems,* published in 1632, led to another summons to the Inquisition, the official church court. A year after this publication Galileo was forced to renounce his belief in the Copernican theory. His book, along with

Forgive Me, Father

" GALILEO, ABJURATION, 1633

As Galileo made more and more discoveries of astronomical phenomena, the less he could believe the Catholic Church's view that the earth was the center of the universe. In 1632 Galileo published a defense of the sun-centered view of the universe in a book called Dialogue of Two World Systems. *He was summoned before the Inquisition, and after a trial of about 6 months, the Church forced him to sign a confession. On June 22, 1633, dressed in white robes, Galileo kneeled before seven Cardinal-Inquisitors and made his confession.*

Despite this statement, Galileo went on to publish another book, Two New Sciences (1638), *which established the foundations of modern physics and engineering.*

I, Galileo, son of the late Vincenzio Galilei of Florence, seventy years of age...swear that I have always believed, and will continue to believe all that the Holy Catholic and Apostolic Church holds, preaches, and teaches...

I have been judged strongly suspected of heresy, in having held and believed that the sun is motionless in the center of the world, and the earth is not the center and moves...

With sincere heart and unfeigned faith, I abjure, curse, and detest the above-named errors and heresies...I swear that in the future I will never again say or assert, orally or in writing, anything that might cause a similar suspicion about me.

Galileo was a prolific writer as well as a scientist. The paper on the floor in this portrait suggests that he tried out, and discarded, different ideas. His provocative style of writing, however, got him into trouble, especially when he declared that the way the universe is constructed, with the sun at its center, "exists in only one, true, real way, that could not be otherwise."

Copernicus's, was put on the list of censored books. In 1633 Galileo was confined to his home outside Florence, where he remained under house arrest until his death in 1642.

CIRCLING THE TRUTH

Scientific support for sun-centered systems could not be stopped, however. Other astronomers all over Europe had been looking into the theory and collecting new data. One man, a Dane named Tycho Brahe, stood above all the rest as the greatest observer of astronomical phenomena of the time. His dedication to nightly observations produced the most accurate data available anywhere in the world. But he did not have the mathematical skill to analyze his own data. In 1600, Brahe invited a rising mathematical star to join him in Prague as an assistant. The young mathematical genius was Johannes Kepler.

Kepler was born in Germany in 1571. He was sent to a Protestant seminary school, where, despite his strong religious beliefs, his fiercely independent nature made him a target for the clergy and the other students. He endured lonely, friendless school years, withdrawing into mathematics for comfort. It was probably a great shock for him when he attended university, first in Maulbroun and then in Tübingen, and was immediately recognized as a genius by his teachers. One teacher introduced Kepler to Copernicus's theories of a sun-centered universe. Kepler felt an immediate connection to those ideas. The Copernican system appealed to Kepler's deep religious beliefs. He believed the sun to be a metaphor for God—everything should revolve around God. It appealed to his mathematical sense as well.

In 1594, just when Kepler was about to become a clergyman, he was offered a job teaching mathematics in Graz, Austria, which he accepted. There was one problem. Kepler was a terrible teacher. He talked to himself. He went off on tangents. No one could follow his lectures. In his second year, not one student signed up for his courses. Kepler, lost in his own mathematical musings, probably never noticed. In 1598, Kepler's teaching days came to an abrupt end. The

Living as he did before the invention of the telescope, the Danish astronomer Tycho Brahe produced the most exact observations ever that used only the naked eye. He described astronomy as "the oldest and most distinguished of all sciences."

local Catholic archduke closed Kepler's school. Protestants were banned from all desirable ways of earning a living. Townspeople were interrogated. The choice was simple— Roman Catholicism or exile. Kepler chose exile, and Tycho Brahe's offer gave him a good opportunity for escape.

Taking Brahe up on his invitation, and following the temptation of consulting all those wonderful records of planetary positions, Kepler moved to Prague. But Kepler's expectations were soon dashed. Brahe was not the studious scientist that Kepler had expected, but a wild and flamboyant character, complete with a metal nose (he had lost his own in a duel). Moreover, Kepler was not to be Brahe's right-hand man, but only one of many assistants, students, relatives, and moochers, all of whom played much harder than they worked. Kepler was once again the outsider, and

The town of Graz, Austria, was built around a high hill with a castle at the top. Johannes Kepler went to study at the university in Graz in 1594. The wall around the town is typical of European towns built in the Middle Ages.

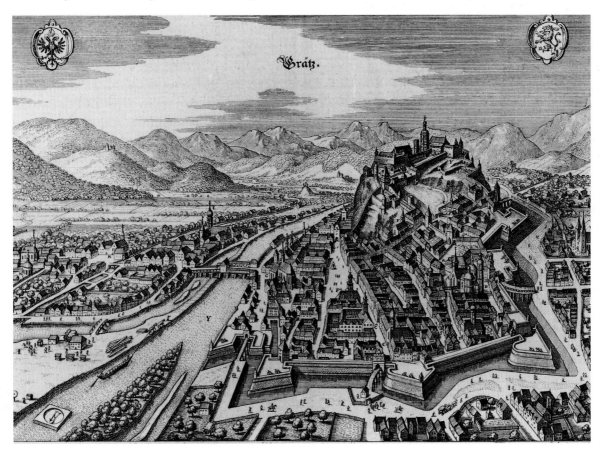

"*D*ay and night I was consumed by the computing, to see whether this idea would agree with the Copernican orbits or if my joy would be carried away by the wind. Within a few days everything worked, and I watched as one body after another fit precisely into its place among the planets."

—Johannes Kepler, letter to Tübinger professor Michael Maestlin, 1595

the target of ridicule. He complained that Brahe was stingy with his data, doling out one kernel at a time, sometimes over dinner, as if in passing. Kepler told friends that even though Brahe possessed the best observations, they were no good without an architect who could put them all to use. Kepler longed to be that architect. But Brahe jealously guarded his life's work. Kepler and Brahe fought constantly. However, each needed the other and so they always made up. It wasn't until 18 months after his arrival, after Brahe's death, that Kepler had full access to Brahe's observations. On his deathbed, Brahe willed his data to Kepler.

Kepler threw himself into Brahe's data—years of observations. Brahe's data on Mars gave him the most trouble. The orbit calculated from the data did not form a circle. Ptolemy, Copernicus, Galileo, Brahe—all the astronomers before him had assumed orbits were circles. After three years of trying to find some way to make Brahe's data on the Martian orbit fit into a circular path, Kepler despaired. God, the Divine Geometer, surely would not have created something imperfect. And yet, he reasoned, the earth was far from perfect. The earth had wars and hunger and poverty and pain. And if the earth could be imperfect, then why not the orbits of planets?

For the next decade, Kepler labored until at last he came up with three astronomical laws. The first two laws were announced in Kepler's great work, the *New Astronomy*, published in 1609. Kepler's first law says that the planetary orbits were not shaped like circles at all, but were ellipses closer to the shape of an egg than a circle. The second law explained why planets move faster when they are closer to the sun.

Many years and lots of calculations later, Kepler came up with his third and final law of planetary motion. He discovered that if you square the time it takes a planet to complete its orbit, then divide that by the cube of its average distance from the sun, you get the same number for all the planets. Kepler described this law in a book called *The Harmonies of the World*. To Kepler, this relationship among the planets, this harmony, proved that the world moved with mathematical certainty. He had not only shifted the

"I wanted to become a theologian, for a long time I was restless. Now, however, behold how through my effort God is being celebrated in astronomy."

—Johannes Kepler, letter to Tübingen professor Michael Maestlin, referring to his first book, *The Secret of the Universe* (1595)

center of the universe, he had shifted the nature of planetary movement from mysticism to mathematics.

Astronomers at last had a strong mathematical argument for a sun-centered system. Together with the discoveries of Copernicus and Galileo, Kepler's work contributed to the birth of modern science. Natural philosophers became increasingly confident of their intellectual ability to understand the mysteries of the natural world. This confidence inspired others to question traditional beliefs, both those based on religious scripture and those based on customary practice. Questioning the world and how it works is part of human nature. No one understood this better than Kepler. In *The Secret of the Universe*, he wrote, "We do not ask for what useful purpose the birds do sing, for song is their pleasure since they were created for singing. Similarly, we ought not to ask why the human mind troubles to fathom the secrets of the heavens."

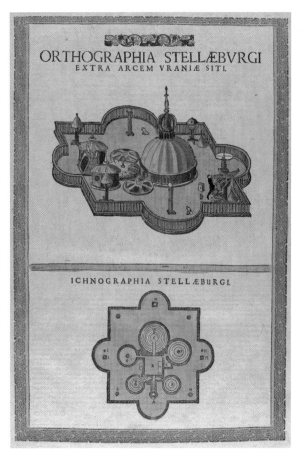

In the 1570s, Tycho Brahe built a castle on the island of Hven, off the coast of Denmark (now part of Sweden). To give his instruments greater stability while he observed the stars, he constructed Stjerneborg, or "castle of the stars," an observatory that was mostly underground.

CHAPTER 7

THE TOOLBOX OF THE ENLIGHTENMENT
THE SCIENTIFIC REVOLUTION

"*The* most beautiful and delightful sight.... Matters of great interest for all observers of natural phenomena... first, from their natural excellence; secondly, from their absolute novelty; and lastly, also on account of the instrument by the aid of which they have been presented to my apprehension."

—Galileo Galilei, on his amazement at what he viewed through the telescope, *The Starry Messenger,* 1610

The making of tools 2 million years ago helped humans move away from their animal selves. The discovery of tools 500 years ago helped humans move again—this time away from superstition and folk wisdom toward science and reason. The foundation had been built centuries before. The ideas were already there—it just took the proper tools to realize them.

When you look at them, tools from millions of years ago may seem quite different than the tools from only a few centuries ago. A rock carved along its edges to create a cutting tool looks primitive next to the polished lenses of telescopes and microscopes. But both serve the same general purpose: to extend the sense organs of humans. Tools launch humans into new dimensions. To cite just one example, think about how computers have changed our lives. Some tools do not even look like tools. Take the language of mathematics, for example. This is a tool that was used to describe the natural world that scientists were seeing through their telescopes and microscopes—a tool that allowed scientists to communicate their ideas to one another.

The leap from watching the night sky with the naked eye to observing it through a telescope is one of history's long jumps. No one knows for sure who invented the telescope, but one story says that it was two Dutch children. The children were playing in a shop that sold eyeglasses and fiddled with the different-shaped lenses. They put two curved lenses together and noticed that when they looked through them, the church weathervane was *huge!* The shopkeeper, Hans Lippershey, had a look for himself. Realizing the potential of such an invention, he set out to protect it. In 1608 he petitioned the Dutch government for a patent—exclusive rights to sell it for the next 30 years—

Galileo constructed many telescopes, each with different abilities to see distant objects. These two are between 4 and 5 feet long. In 1611, Galileo took a new telescope to Venice, where he showed that ships out in the sea could be seen with his telescope "two hours before" they were visible to the naked eye sailing into the harbor.

in an effort to prevent anyone from copying his "instrument for seeing at a distance," as he called it. In the meantime, word of the invention spread to other countries. Soon, despite Lippershey's patent, telescopes were soon being sold all over Paris.

At first no one believed the images they saw through the telescope. People thought they could trust only what they saw directly with their own eyes. Mirrors, prisms, and lenses created lies and were all about trickery. Even Galileo, one of the great astronomers of the era, double-checked the authenticity of the telescope when he first started working with it. He would look through his telescope at an object and then walk over to it and examine it closely. He tested his telescope, which he made himself, for two years, and in 1610 he wrote that he had tested his instrument in "hundreds of thousands of experiments, involving thousands and thousands of objects, near and far, large and small, bright and dark; hence I do not see how it can enter the mind of anyone that I have simple-mindedly remained deceived by my observations."

While everyone else thought the "instrument for seeing at a distance" might be useful for battles and travel, Galileo turned it toward the sky. What he saw changed the way we view our place in the universe. He confirmed that the Milky Way was actually made up of stars clustered together, not a star "exhaling" as people had thought, comparing its foggy appearance to their own breath on a cold night. And the

A compound microscope, like this example from about 1680, has two magnifying lenses; the closest to the object being studied is called the objective and the other is the eyepiece. This is the type of microscope that Marcello Malpighi used in his observations of tiny biological specimens, such as the lung tissue and trachea of a frog.

moon was not a glass ball full of smoke—it had mountains and craters just like the earth. Could plants be growing on the moon, with animals grazing, and maybe even people looking back at us?

What astonished Galileo the most was that moons circled Jupiter while Jupiter circled the sun. What if our sun circled something even larger while we circled the sun? Just by having scientists look through the telescope and report their findings, the idea of our universe went from something we thought we could see to something limited only by our imaginations.

Galileo's imagination spurred him to use his telescope as a microscope. He told a visitor in 1614, "I have seen flies which look as big as lambs, and have learned that they are covered with hair and have very pointed nails." The critics who did not trust what was seen through a telescope, an instrument that made faraway things seem closer, had the same wariness for the microscope, which made small things seem bigger. There were practical uses for the telescope—for example, you could spy on your enemy on the next hill. But what possible use did a microscope serve? This could only be an instrument of the devil, designed to trick the God-given senses.

Marcello Malpighi was an Italian physician who became the personal physician of Pope Innocent XII. Malpighi did not think his microscope—commonly called a "flea glass" because its early users observed fleas with it—was an instrument of the devil. He wrote in a letter to his friend, "[M]icroscopical observation reveals things even more wonderful" than he was capable of seeing with his eyes alone. Malpighi was an extremely careful person who worked long hours in his Bologna laboratory day after day, always recording the results of his observations of biological specimens. He spent untold hours trying to understand how blood moved through the body. At the time, there were many theories about blood flow. A popular one had the blood flowing through the arteries to the outer part of the body during waking hours, then back to the core of the body through the veins while the person slept.

Malpighi was partial to a theory he had studied while in medical school. The theory put forth by the British physician William Harvey was not widely accepted, but it made sense to Malpighi. Harvey had concluded that the blood traveled through the body several times a day and had figured out that the heart was like a pump, but there was still a missing link. Harvey knew that new blood was created too slowly to make up a fresh batch for several circulations in a day, so how was the old blood "refreshed"? Malpighi and

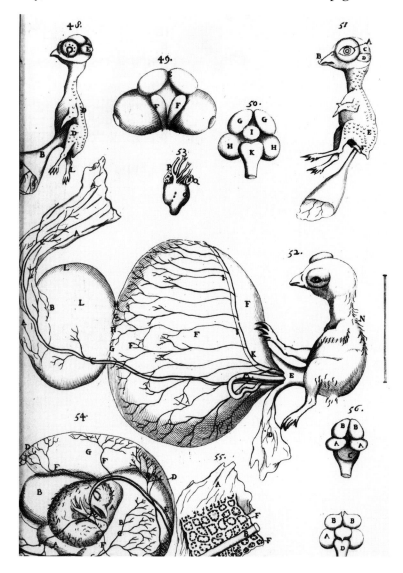

Marcello Malpighi was an excellent illustrator and was the first scientist to produce detailed drawings of the formation of a chick in an egg.

"We have as much right to call this movement of the blood circular as Aristotle had to say that the air and rain emulate the circular movement of the heavenly bodies. . . . This organ [the heart] deserves to be styled the starting point of life and the sun of our microcosm just as much as the sun deserves to be styled the heart of the world."

—William Harvey, *On the Motion of the Heart and of Blood in Animals*, 1628

his flea glass found the answer. As he used the microscope to examine the exposed lungs of a frog, Malpighi was able to actually see the blood pulsing through very small tubes, or capillaries, connecting the arteries and the veins of the frog. This was an astounding revelation, for it was the missing link in William Harvey's discovery that the blood circulates from the heart through the arteries and then back to the heart through the veins.

Before then, no one had actually seen this flow of blood. With Malpighi's observations, it was now clear that Harvey's theory of blood circulation was true, and that this little magnifying device could be used to make the *invisible* structures of life visible. Galileo pointed the telescope at the infinite, Malpighi pointed the microscope at the infinitesimal, and everyone's view of the world was broadening as a result.

FINDING THE WAY

By the early 17th century, the tools for travel were also advancing thanks to an emerging science called cartography, or mapmaking. The new techniques of cartography were so mathematically complicated they had to be formally taught. Sailors could not just pick them up on the job, while piloting a ship. By the end of the 15th century, compass markings on a map were represented by a symbol called a rose because the points of the compass look like flower petals. Originally these petals represented the so-called four winds from the north, south, east, and west; but as directions became more precise, the petals were cut in half three times, until there were 32 points in all.

Maps in the 16th century contained meridian lines. Meridian lines circle the globe through the North and South poles. Because flat maps have to represent a curved world—the earth—these lines curved. Since the lines bunched up near the poles, this area of a map was often difficult to read. And if those lines were not accurately drawn, a ship could find itself way off course.

To solve this problem, a Flemish mapmaker named Gerhard Kremer (or Mercator, the Latin name by which he became known) developed a more precise and readable way to represent a curved world on a flat surface. Rather than having the meridian lines meet at the poles, he drew them as parallel lines. To do so, he had to distort the area near the poles, widening it so that his north-south lines remained parallel. His map design, where the surface of the globe is "projected" onto a flat map, is known today as a Mercator projection.

From the late 16th century on, navigators used Mercator projection maps on their way to America and other places around the globe. To chart a course with these new tools meant using a rose with its compass points and then drawing a line with a constant compass bearing that represented the path of the ship. This compass line was called a "rhumb line." (The word *rhumb* comes from the Greek word *rhombus*, a geometric figure with four sides of equal length and opposite sides parallel to one another.) By checking the

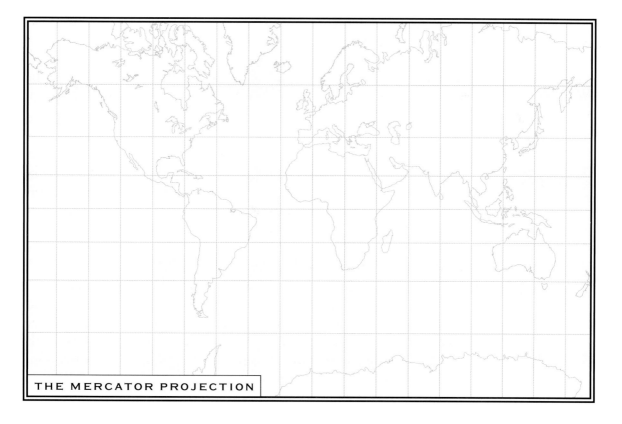

THE MERCATOR PROJECTION

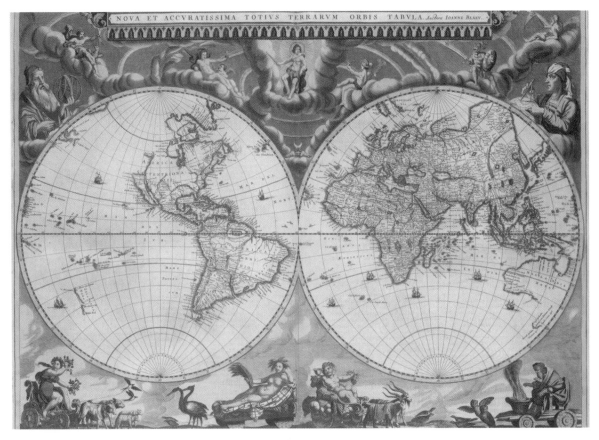

This world map, made by a Dutch mapmaker in about 1620, does not use a Mercator projection. As a result, the horizontal latitude and vertical longitude lines, used to locate any place on the globe, are spaced farther apart at the equator and closer together at the poles to compensate for the earth's curved surface. This feature made this map and others like it difficult for sailors to use as navigational tools.

rhumb line on the Mercator projection map, navigators could check the angle at which their ship crossed each of the meridians, thus keeping themselves from veering off course. Using these navigation tools, trading companies and adventurers found their way to new as well as old places without getting lost.

METHODS TO THEIR MADNESS

Galileo's tests on the telescope illustrated a whole new way of looking at the world—of examining what was true. Natural philosophers (as scientists called themselves back then) began to perform experiments in such a way that the experiment could be repeated by others and the results compared—and discussed. Many people think that the scientific revolution came about because of new technology and the discoveries

Burning Bright

> **JOSEPH PRIESTLEY, EXPERIMENTS AND OBSERVATIONS ON DIFFERENT KINDS OF GASES, 1776**

Joseph Priestley, an English scientist, laid the foundation for the science we now call chemistry. He is best known for his experiments with gases. In 1776 he published Experiments and Observations on Different Kinds of Gases, *which described experiments he had made the previous year. In the experiment described here, Priestley discovered oxygen. When he placed a lit candle in a glass container, he expected the particular gas he had collected to put the flame out. Instead the flame grew brighter. Priestley felt that further investigation of this "new" gas was needed.*

Still, however, having no conception of the real cause of this phenomenon, I considered it as something very extraordinary...I particularly remember my telling [a colleague] that I was myself perfectly satisfied of its being common air, as it appeared to be so by the test of nitrous air; though, for the satisfaction of others, I wanted a mouse to make the proof quite complete.

On the 8th of this month I procured a mouse, and put it into a glass vessel, containing two ounce-measures of the air from mercurius calcinatus [mercury oxide, a red powder]. Had it been common air, a full-grown mouse, as this was, would have lived in it about a quarter of an hour. In this air, however, my mouse lived a full hour; and though it was taken out seemingly dead, it appeared to have been only exceedingly chilled; for, upon being held to the fire, it presently revived, and appeared not to have received any harm from the experiment.

This 1791 cartoon of Joseph Priestley shows him stepping on the Bible and holding other "inflammatory" literature. Priestley was both a scientist who discovered oxygen and a deeply religious believer who nonetheless criticized religious officials.

that followed, but the real revolution was in *how* these natural philosophers looked at the world. The answers did not create the revolution; the questions did. Begin by doubting *everything,* set up experiments, observe what happens, record your results, and repeat, repeat, repeat... Then talk with others who have conducted the same experiments. What were their results? By removing all bias, that is, prejudiced judgments, the new scientific method enabled a more accurate picture of the world to emerge. This was yet another tool.

In the very beginning of the 17th century, an 8-year-old boy named René Descartes entered a Jesuit school in Anjou, France. There Descartes was taught the importance of *method.* Unlike the universities of the time, which required their students to memorize book after book and called that learning, the Jesuits valued *how* you studied even more than what you studied. For Descartes the *when* was a little unusual, too. His health was poor and so he was allowed to sleep in every morning until 11 o'clock. It was a practice he continued for most of the rest of his life. He told other natural philosophers that the only way to do math well was to stay in bed all morning.

While he lay in bed in the mornings, he meditated on the right way to study the sciences. Descartes believed the only pure subject was mathematics. Mathematics was his chosen tool. He began writing a book (which he never finished) called *Rules for the Direction of the Mind.* He wanted to understand how we know if something is true. How do we tell truth and fiction apart? What if our entire universe is just a big lie? How do we know that mathematics is true and not something conjured by the devil?

Since Descartes couldn't prove anything, he stopped believing in anything. He refused to accept a single thing as true. If you want to build a solid foundation, he argued in the many books and papers he did publish, you must first strip everything away. But what comes next? Where do you go from nothing at all? If you stop believing in everything, including mathematics, what tools do you use to build a solid structure on which to base your thinking? There must be something that is certain to exist! Was it during one of those morning meditations that the thought struck Descartes? *Cogito, ergo sum*—"I think, therefore I am." The very fact that he was thinking proved that he existed. If he did not exist, he would not be thinking.

Descartes needed to think. He had established himself as an exceptional mathematician. He was known for his original work in physics. And his work, which took philosophy in a whole new direction using the "new" sciences, made him so sought-after that it was hard for him to find the privacy necessary to continue his meditations. His success had come as something of a mixed blessing. So he moved to Holland and lived in seclusion. As soon as people discovered where he was, he would move somewhere else to keep out of the public eye.

For 20 years he hid and thought and wrote, coming out into the world only on rare occasions. But then, in 1649, Queen Christina of Sweden summoned Descartes to serve as her philosophy teacher. Unaware of (or perhaps indifferent to) her new instructor's need to stay in bed late, she scheduled their lessons at 5:00 a.m. Maybe Descartes had been right all those years about staying in bed late, because in 1650, he caught pneumonia and died at the age of 53.

His body was shipped from Sweden back to France, but not all of it made it home. Relic collectors along the way stole bits and pieces of his body. He may have returned to France diminished in size, but his reputation was larger than life. Despite his life work of separating reason from religion, many Catholics felt Descartes should be given the honor of sainthood.

Others, before and after Descartes, tried to design a foolproof method for arriving at scientific truths. One of the most enthusiastic was Sir Francis

After finishing his university training, the French philosopher René Descartes traveled around Europe to see how other Europeans lived. In 1626, he was seen in Paris by a scholar who described Descartes as "a little well-built figure, modestly clad in green… and only wearing sword and feather in token of his quality as a gentleman." In this portrait, Descartes (standing at the table) gives a lecture on geometry attended by Queen Christina (center), who summoned him to Sweden to be her philosophy teacher.

Francis Bacon's importance as a political official in the government of Queen Elizabeth I of England made him a subject of portrait artists. Bacon's contributions to science were not in the form of discoveries; instead, he promoted the scientific method, a new way of approaching scientific experimentation.

Bacon. Bacon was a gifted writer born in 1561 to a wealthy and well-connected family in London. At a time when it was unusual for women to be educated, his mother learned Latin and Greek as well as French and Italian. At the very young age of 12, Francis Bacon was sent to Trinity College, part of Cambridge University. When his father died, leaving the family penniless, he returned home to support his family by practicing law. When Queen Elizabeth I appointed him Lord Treasurer in 1572, Bacon became one of the most powerful men in England.

Although Bacon made no original scientific discoveries, he was influential in the way we think about science. An amateur scientist, he had an infectious enthusiasm and optimism about the pursuit of science. Bacon argued that science was important, not just for the sake of knowledge, but to improve the human condition. He called for a completely new beginning in science that he called "The Great Instauration"—the great new beginning.

Bacon urged natural philosophers "to try the whole thing anew upon a better plan, and to commence a total reconstruction of science, arts, and all human knowledge, raised upon the proper foundations." The ancient writings that had held up for so long were starting to crumble under the weight of new scientific discoveries. One of these, the Greek philosopher Aristotle's collected writings called the *Organon,* had guided Europeans for centuries. The *Organon,* named for a Greek word meaning "instrument," is a set of principles used in scientific or philosophical investigation. So Bacon chose to call the work that described his intellectual philosophy *The New Organon.*

Like Descartes, Bacon tried to come up with a scientific method that cleansed the mind of bias, or prejudiced judgments. According to Bacon there are four kinds of biases, or "idols." These are the Idols of the Tribe, the Idols of the Cave, the Idols of the Market-Place, and the Idols of the Theater. The Idols of the Tribe are simply the prejudices common to human beings in general (the tribe). Perhaps our senses lead us astray, or we jump to conclusions based on wishful thinking or failure to think things through. The Idols of the Cave are peculiar to each of us as individuals (in our caves). Everyone owns a set of biases and prejudices that influences his or her thinking. The Idols of the Market-Place come from the limitations of language. We might use certain words (out in the marketplace) or apply labels without thinking or out of habit. The Idols of the Theater are those outdated ideas we hold onto long after they have lost their usefulness and those false assumptions (the theater can mislead you!) that come from misinterpreting experiments.

Bacon believed that prejudices put mental blinders on people, preventing them from seeing the truth and making objective observations. The first step in his renewed scientific method was to rid the mind of all these biases. At the same time, he hoped to build a logical system that would overcome human limitations. For Bacon, it was all about the scientific experiment. He argued that "the experiment itself shall judge of the thing." Bacon's emphasis on "experiment" as the path to truth struck a chord with others who began their own examinations of how we acquire knowledge.

The title page from Francis Bacon's book The Great New Beginning, *about the birth of a new scientific era, shows a ship sailing through a gate. It suggests that mankind is setting off into an unexplored sea of new knowledge. A Latin inscription at the bottom of the page is taken from the Bible. It says, "Many will pass through and knowledge will be increased."*

THE APPLE OF HIS EYE

The year Descartes died, an 8-year-old future toolmaker was attending a village school in England. His tool, like Descartes's, would also be mathematics, but he would take it in another direction. His name was Isaac Newton.

Newton was a lonely young boy whose father had died only months before his birth. When his widowed mother remarried, she moved to a nearby village and left him to live with his grandparents. Newton missed his mother dread-

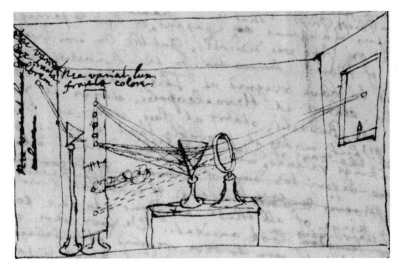

A sketch by Isaac Newton illustrates an experiment with light and its various colors and how they are affected by prisms. Light enters the room through a small hole in a window shutter (right) and passes through a prism (on table, right). A beam of colored light from the prism then passes through another prism and is reflected on the wall behind it. The experiment showed that the color of light was not changed as it passed through the prisms.

fully. When he was sent away to school at 12, he kept to himself, not making friends with the other children. Like many great thinkers, Newton began by tinkering. One person in town recalled that after school, Newton "busied himself in making knickknacks and wood models in many kinds: for which purpose he had got little saws, hatchets, hammers and a whole shop of tools." The inspiration for one model came from watching the construction of a windmill. Newton built his own miniature version, complete with a "miller" played by a pet mouse. When the mouse reached for a kernel of corn, wheels and gears began to turn, setting the windmill's blades into motion.

In 1661, Newton enrolled at King's College, Cambridge, where he quickly became absorbed in the study of the classics, logic, history, and many other subjects. His interests were broad, and he began to keep notebooks—stacks of them. In some of his notebooks his writing was neat and precise. In others he scribbled as if he could not keep pace with his thoughts. The notebooks had headings for the various topics he planned to study, ranging from "Time and Eternity" and "Matter" to "Air," "Earth," and "Sleep." Newton was interested in everything.

He thought a lot about some topics, and less about others, but one of the topics he thought about most was how to look at the world. Just like Descartes, Newton had been taught to believe what he could see, hear, smell, touch, or taste was true, and like Descartes, Newton instinctively distrusted these five senses. Newton embraced the new approach to questioning nature—he gathered data, formulated a hypothesis, or theory, conducted experiments, and then attempted to validate or reject the hypothesis. He sought the truth by way of the new scientific method.

Newton shared another of Descartes's habits as well: he liked to be alone with his thoughts. Later in life, when he was asked how he had come to so much original thought, he said, "Truth is the offspring of silence and unbroken meditation." One of the most productive periods of his life was brought on by a tragedy in the city where he lived. In 1665, the plague was sweeping through London and surrounding areas, and as many as 8,000 people a week were dying. Londoners were fleeing the city by the thousands. Cambridge University closed its doors, and Newton was forced to return to his rural hometown until the danger passed. Newton found himself isolated, with hours and hours for silence and meditation.

Newton believed that the universe could be explained by mathematics, but he was frustrated with his toolkit. Algebra was fine for figuring out the value of an unknown in a specific equation, and geometry was fine for figuring out areas and volumes. But how could he describe mathematically objects that moved about—and moved about erratically? Descartes had solved a few individual problems of this kind, but his methods were long and tedious and could not be used for general applications. Newton needed a new math, a math that would work with objects that constantly changed their speed. In 1666, before his 24th birthday, he found a way. He called his method "fluxions." We call it calculus. With it, Newton could describe the arc of a planet's orbit and describe the speed with which the planet hurtles through space. And even the tiniest variations in this planet's movement could be computed using his fluxions. He now had the language to describe

At the end of Isaac Newton's life, he said, "I do not know what I may appear to the world; but to myself I seem to have been only like a boy, playing on the seashore…diverting myself in now and then finding a smoother pebble or prettier shell than ordinary, while the great ocean of truth lay all undiscovered before me."

"Every body continues in its state of rest, or of uniform motion in a straight line, unless it is compelled to change that state by forces impressed upon it."

—Newton's first law, *Principia*, 1687

"*S*o intent, so serious upon his studies that he eat very sparingly, nay ofttimes he has forgot to eat at all. He very rarely went to Bed till 2 or 3 of the clock, sometimes not till 5 or 6, ... the fire scarcely going out either Night or Day, he sitting up one Night ... till he had finished his Chymicall Experiments, in ye Performance of which he was the most acurate, strict, exact."

—Humphrey Newton, on his employer and distant relative Issac Newton, in a letter to John Conduitt, 1728

to other scientists how the universe operated in a rational and predictable way.

It was also during this time that Newton made the apple famous for something other than pies. While he was thinking in the garden under the shade of a few apple trees, an apple fell to the ground. Newton, being in a contemplative mood, wondered why "attraction at a distance" (which we now call gravity) did not seem to disappear no matter how far you got from the center of the earth. It pulls whether you are standing on the tallest building or the highest mountain. Surely it must also pull on the moon. Maybe—just maybe—that is what keeps the moon in orbit around the earth. And if that force is what keeps the moon circling the earth, maybe the sun has the same force that keeps the earth and all the other planets circling it.

Newton was very familiar with Galileo's and Descartes's theories that once a body is in motion, it will stay in motion until an outside force changes things, and incorporated these theories into his own. He also knew that a body in motion moves in a straight line unless it is acted upon by something else. Therefore, if Newton were to throw an apple, it would continue in a straight line away from the earth—that is, if it weren't for gravity. Newton wondered what would happen if he had superhuman strength and could throw the apple *really* far. He imagined the moon as a giant falling apple. The apple tries to travel in a straight line, but the earth keeps tugging on it. The balance between the straight-line path and the downward pull is perfect, keeping the "apple" moon in orbit around the earth.

Like many other natural philosophers of his time, Newton believed in the so-called wisdom of the ancients. Natural philosophers believed that the great truths of nature were known in ancient times by the great thinkers, as well as the most important people in the Bible—King Solomon, the prophet Isaiah, and Jesus of Nazareth. The idea was that these brilliant men had written their knowledge in a secret code for only the worthy to discover. If you looked hard enough, every aspect of the physical phenomenon of the universe could be explained. Newton studied the Old and New

Testaments so deeply that he could more than hold his own with the clergy. Scholars estimate that he wrote 1.4 million words on religion, more than on any other subject—more than on mathematics, physics, or astronomy. He saw no conflict between science and religion. His view of the universe included God as a necessary part.

During those two years at home avoiding the plague, alone with his meditations and his notebooks, Newton made discovery after discovery. He became so lost in his work he often forgot to eat and rarely went to bed until the wee hours, often not until dawn. Even though Newton is heralded today as one of the greatest scientists of all time, he remained fixed on what he had yet to learn. Not long before he died at 84, he said, "I do not know what I may appear to the world; but to myself I seem to have been only like a boy, playing on the seashore, and diverting myself in now and then finding a smoother pebble or a prettier shell than ordinary, while the great ocean of truth lay all undiscovered before me."

In the early 17th century, Europe was bursting with new ideas. Many of these ideas drew upon the spirit of the scientific revolution. By the middle of the 18th century, that revolution had made its way into the minds of poets and ordinary people. The English poet Alexander Pope wrote,

> Nature and Nature's laws lay hidden in night.
> God said, Let Newton be! And all was light.

This brave idea—that scientists could suddenly understand all things—encouraged other thinkers to be bold in their thinking, too.

Isaac Newton presented this reflecting telescope to the Royal Society of London in 1671. He was the first person to make a reflecting telescope, which reflects light using a mirror, that actually worked.

CHAPTER 8

BOLD IDEAS AND PRISON SENTENCES
THE LITERARY LIFE

Some people always seem to find trouble. Perhaps you know a student who has to serve detention every afternoon, for example. François-Marie Arouet, later known as Voltaire, was that type of person. He was arrested, thrown in prison, or exiled so many times he kept money stashed for quick getaways. He just couldn't help himself—he was the Enlightenment equivalent of the wise-guy.

Voltaire had been born to a wealthy, but not noble, family in Paris in 1694. To appear as if he were indeed from a noble family, he added "de Voltaire" to his name. The "de" was meant to signify a noble birth. When a real noble-man sarcastically asked Voltaire, "Monsieur de Voltaire, Monsieur Arouet, exactly what is your name?" Voltaire snapped, "I myself do not bear a great name, but *I* know how to *honor* the one I carry." That was a big mistake. Insulting the French nobility was dangerous. A few days later, two thugs attacked Voltaire and beat him up, while the nobleman Voltaire had insulted sat in his carriage and watched. Legend has it the nobleman called out to the thugs, "Don't hit him in the head, something good may come out of it."

Voltaire's father wanted him to become a lawyer, but Voltaire had other things in mind. He wanted to be a writer. His father complained that he would never make a decent living doing anything so frivolous. It wouldn't be long before Voltaire would prove his father wrong. By the time he was 40, he was well known and, thanks to a few good investments, very well off. Voltaire wrote extensively. He tried every type of writing—plays, novels, short stories, essays, poems, book reviews, scientific papers, and more than 20,000 letters. Some of those letters would get him into trouble—again.

Voltaire seems very pleased with himself as he holds his provocative book La Henriade, *which describes the persecutions caused by religious belief, including Catholicism. He wrote the long poem while being held in the infamous French prison called the Bastille.*

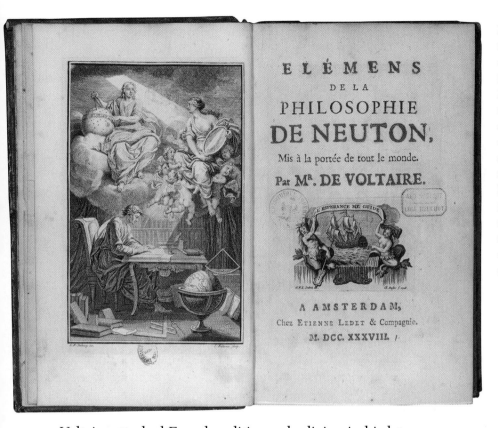

ELÉMENS
DE LA
PHILOSOPHIE
DE NEUTON,
Mis à la portée de tout le monde.
Par Mʳ. DE VOLTAIRE.

A AMSTERDAM,
Chez Etienne Ledet & Compagnie.
M. DCC. XXXVIII.

Not just a political thinker, Voltaire was also such an enthusiastic supporter of Isaac Newton's scientific theories that he wrote a book called Elements of Newton's Philosophy. *Voltaire accepted the idea that all physical bodies, from rocks and trees to planets and stars, pulled at each other with gravitational attraction, even at great distances.*

Voltaire attacked French politics and religion in his letters, and the French government did not take the criticism well. Government officials ordered Voltaire thrown into prison. Voltaire had already been to the Bastille twice (once for insulting that nobleman), and he was far from eager to return. So he fled to England. If you were critical of the king and the church in France, you must live with your bags packed. But for crusaders against injustice and intolerance in 18th-century Europe, England was the place to be. "How I love everything English!" Voltaire wrote home to a female friend, "How I love these people who say what they think!" Voltaire admired the political freedom in England. He wrote in his *Philosophical Dictionary,*

> See what the laws of England have achieved: they
> have restored to every man his natural rights,
> from which nearly all monarchies have despoiled
> him. These rights are: full freedom of person and

"*T*he institution of religion exists only to keep mankind in order, and to make men merit the goodness of God by their virtue. Everything in a religion which does not extend toward this goal must be considered alien or dangerous."

—Voltaire, *Philosophical Dictionary*, 1764

property; to speak to the nation through his pen; to be judged in criminal matters by a jury of free men; to be judged in any matter only according to precise law; [and] to profess in peace whatever religion he prefers.

In France at that time, the king Louis XV and the Catholic Church held all the power. It was a case of mutual support. The church taught the people that God gave the king the right to determine what was right and what was wrong. Therefore the king's word was law. In return, the king supported the authority of the Catholic Church. So long as the people believed in the "divine right of kings," noblemen and clergy could keep their privileged positions. No wonder they did not like Voltaire stirring things up. Someone as witty and clever as Voltaire writing about reform was a threat to the good thing they had going.

Of course, the French didn't make it easy for Voltaire. To publish something in France, it first had to be approved by the official censors. The censors analyzed every word to be sure there was nothing contrary to king or church. Any

The English painter William Hogarth depicts the many kinds of people who show up at polling places to cast their votes. His characters have various problems; one cannot walk and another seems unable to read the news. The man with the long wig seems to be protesting the qualifications of the peg-legged man waiting in front of the counter to cast his vote. Despite the potential drawbacks, however, Voltaire was impressed by the political freedom that the English enjoyed.

"The sovereign…has no right to use coercion to lead men to religion, which in its nature presupposes choice and liberty."

—Voltaire, *Philosophical Dictionary*, 1764

book published without the censors' approval was burned by the public executioner, and the printer and writer were thrown in jail. As a result, lots of Voltaire's work went up in smoke. To avoid being thrown in prison—again—Voltaire wrote anonymously. He disguised his criticisms by placing his stories in ancient times, made-up places, and foreign countries. His readers called him the Genius of Mockery. Through his clever humor Voltaire unmasked the evils of French society.

IMAGINARY FRIENDS——A USEFUL TOOL

Voltaire was not the only French writer who used letters to criticize the government and the church. A very clever nobleman by the name of Baron de Montesquieu used the literary device of imaginary "Persian Letters" to criticize and poke fun at many French and European customs. Montesquieu was born into a wealthy aristocratic family in 1689. His father was a judge who made sure that his son also studied law—no wriggling out of work for Montesquieu. After that training, Montesquieu became a lawyer and a member of the French parliament.

Montesquieu invented a series of letters from two imaginary Persian visitors to various people back home. They had made the long journey overland to Paris, writing letters along the way that portrayed French manners and customs through their eyes. In one letter, the imaginary Persian named Rica wrote of the king of France and the Christian pope. He called them "magicians" because they could persuade people to believe many surprising things. The king could persuade his subjects to believe that "a piece of paper is money." This phrase cleverly revealed Montesquieu's

Montesquieu's Persian Letters, originally published in 1721, was a best-seller in France that went through many editions, including this one from 1873. The book criticized European culture, especially French culture, using the words of fictitious Middle Easterners who had traveled to France and observed its customs.

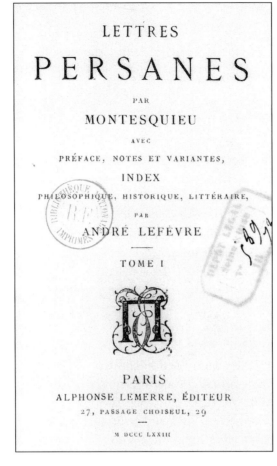

LETTRES

PERSANES

PAR

MONTESQUIEU

AVEC

PRÉFACE, NOTES ET VARIANTES,

INDEX

PHILOSOPHIQUE, HISTORIQUE, LITTÉRAIRE,

PAR

ANDRÉ LEFÈVRE

TOME I

PARIS

ALPHONSE LEMERRE, ÉDITEUR

27, PASSAGE CHOISEUL, 29

M DCCC LXXIII

doubts about the value of paper money compared to gold or silver coins. When Montesquieu wanted to take a closer look at the widespread European belief that "the king's touch" could actually cure people of disease, he merely had his Persian character marvel at the persuasive powers of someone who could convince others that "he cures all kinds of disease, simply by touching them."

The pope, the Persian visitors claimed, was "an even greater magician." He "makes the prince believe that three is only one, or that the bread he eats is not bread, or that wine drunk is not wine." Montesquieu, like Newton and other deeply religious philosophers of the time, questioned the church's doctrine of one God in three divine figures—God the Father, Jesus the Son, and the Holy Spirit. For Newton, worshipping three figures violated the Bible's first commandment, which states there shall be only one God. While Newton preferred to keep his beliefs to himself, Montesquieu wanted people to ask questions. He wanted them to question the idea that wine and bread used in the Catholic Mass were transformed into the body and blood of Christ. So Montesquieu used a technique every writer knows—if you want your reader to question something, have a character in your work question it.

One question Montesquieu thought about was whether history happened by accident or if it was guided by *causes*. He studied ancient history to find the answer. He wrote,

Goodness and Government

MONTESQUIEU, THE SPIRIT OF THE LAWS, 1748

In The Spirit of the Laws, *published in 1748, Montesquieu wrote in a far more serious tone than he had in* The Persian Letters. *Instead of making fun of French customs, he took a critical look at governments. He spoke of virtue as the love of law and love of your country. He argued that a government could and should change depending on the circumstances. That idea may not seem terribly "enlightened" to you, but in the 18th century, the idea that king and crown need not be permanent was shocking.*

On republican government and on laws relative to democracy

In a republic when the people as a body have sovereign power, it is a *Democracy.* When the sovereign power is in the hands of a part of the people, it is called an *aristocracy.*

In a democracy the people are, in certain respects, the monarchs; in other respects, they are the subjects... Therefore, the laws establishing the right to vote are fundamental in this government. Indeed, it is as important in this case to regulate how, by who, for whom, and on what issues votes should be cast, as it is in a monarchy to know the monarch and how he should govern...

There need not be much integrity for a monarchical or despotic government to maintain or sustain itself. The force of the laws in the one and the prince's ever-raised arm in the other can rule or contain the whole. But in a popular state there must be an additional spring, which is VIRTUE.

This portrait of Montesquieu presents him in profile, the style often used to portray great Roman and Greek statesmen. Montesquieu was impressed by the English form of government, and his insightful understanding of it led an English official to say, "You have understood us better than we understand ourselves."

It is not Fortune who governs the world, as we see from the history of the Romans...there are general causes, moral or physical, which operate in every monarchy, raise it, maintain it, or overwhelm it. All that occurs is subject to these causes; and if a particular cause, like the accidental result of a battle, has ruined a state, there was a general cause which made the downfall of this state ensue from a single battle.

For Montesquieu, history was not just a collection of random events controlled by the whim of God. It was a flow of events patterned by rules and laws. If he could just discover the pattern, Montesquieu believed, that knowledge would improve the quality of society and human life.

Montesquieu studied governments in order to find relationships, especially between forms of law and types of government. He divided all the political systems he studied into three types. There were monarchies, governments ruled by kings and queens. There were despotisms, governments ruled by dictators. And there were republics, governments ruled by leaders elected by the people.

Montesquieu had no doubt: a government elected by the people was the best form of government. But for a republic to succeed, Montesquieu recognized there had to be a balance of power. Montesquieu's ideal government may sound familiar: a democracy divided into three branches: executive, legislative, and judicial. This "separation of powers," as Montesquieu called it, prevented any one person or group from getting too much power. Montesquieu's plan was similar to the English system, but instead of a king or queen heading the executive branch, an elected official would be in charge. Montesquieu's ideas eventually became the foundation for the Constitution of the United States. According to the U.S. Constitution, the president and vice president, and various officials the president appoints, form the executive branch; the Congress, composed of the Senate and the House of Representatives, is the legislative branch, writing the laws; and the Supreme Court and the lower courts serve as the judicial branch, interpreting the laws.

"*I*t is true, that in democracies the people seem to do what they please; but political liberty does not consist in an unrestrained freedom. In governments, that is, in societies directed by laws, liberty can consist only in the power of doing what we ought to will, and in not being constrained to do what we ought not to will."

—Baron de Montesquieu,
The Spirit of the Laws, 1748

The U.S. Constitution was completed in September 1787 and ratified, or made into law, in June 1788. It was based in part on Montesquieu's political theories as well as those of John Locke. It begins by stating that this new government was being established to "form a more perfect union, establish justice, insure domestic tranquility, provide for the common defence, promote the general welfare, and to secure the blessings of liberty."

IT ALL ADDS UP

As the 18th century progressed, a vast new body of knowledge accumulated. Scientists had made lots of discoveries in astronomy, chemistry, medicine, geography, physics, and electricity. Reports of exciting and exotic cultures and societies from explorers and travelers who had visited distant lands flooded in. Voltaire's and Montesquieu's writings about political authority, who should rule, and the rights of citizens sparked debates that made everyone question existing governments and look for better ways to govern.

In his description of the Encyclopédie, *Dénis Diderot noted that "all things must be examined, debated, investigated without exception and without regard for anyone's feelings." He felt that people needed to stop relying on old teachings and make and share new discoveries, which the* Encyclopédie *set out to do.*

Someone needed to collect all this knowledge. Someone needed to bring all this new knowledge together in a single book. The great medieval and modern tradition of the "encyclopedia" was the obvious choice. The name comes from a Greek word that means "cycle of education," and it referred to a book designed to contain the wisdom needed for a well-rounded education.

By 1728 the British had published their "cyclopedia," the *Universal Dictionary of Arts and Sciences*. French intellectuals wanted a French translation of this book. But after bickering with a potential translator, the deal broke off, and the French decided to write their own version—a much larger version. The English encyclopedia had neglected anatomy, as well as history and geography. The French editors planned an entirely new encyclopedia. It was to be a revolutionary book that would allow everyone access to knowledge that only kings, sultans, and an educated few had access to before. In the words of its editor, Dénis Diderot, it was to be a grand book, an effort "to collect all the knowledge scattered over the face of the earth, to present its general outlines and structure to the men with whom we live, and to transmit this to those who will come after us."

The task of organizing and editing this great work, called the *Encyclopédie*, and subtitled *A Systematic Dictionary of Science, Arts, and the Trades*, was assigned to Diderot by a Paris publisher, Le Breton. Like Voltaire, Diderot often found himself in trouble. He, too, had been to jail for his liberal thinking. "No man has received from nature the

It could only belong to a philosophical age to attempt an encyclopedia; and I have said this because such a work constantly demands more intellectual daring than is commonly found in ages of pusillanimous [cowardly] taste.

—Jean Le Rond d'Alembert, *Encyclopédie*, 1751

right of commanding others," wrote Diderot in an article criticizing the king's power. His idea that information should be available to everyone was not very popular with the French government, either. They tried to prevent the *Encyclopédie* from being published, but Diderot was passionate about the project. Then again, Diderot was passionate about everything—even his portrait. Artists who painted his portrait could not capture the many facets of his personality to his satisfaction. He once complained, "I had a hundred different expressions in a day, according to the mood that was on me. I was serene, sad, dreamy, tender, violent, passionate, eager. The outward signs of my many and varying states of mind chased one another so rapidly across my face that the painter's eye caught a different me from moment to moment, and never got one right."

Diderot and his coworkers tackled the momentous task of collecting and recording all the knowledge in every field. His team labored for more than 20 years, until in 1772 they had 28 volumes. The encyclopedia featured 11 volumes filled with illustrations of machines and technology that revealed the secrets of tanning, printing, and other trades in vivid

The leading figures of the Enlightenment who created the French Encyclopédie, *including Voltaire (center, with arm raised) and Diderot (to the right of Voltaire), engage in serious discussions at the dinner table.*

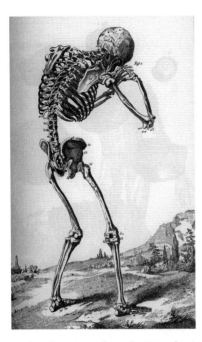

In this illustration from the Encyclo-pédie, *the bones of the body are carefully drawn and labeled with numbers. It is similar to contemporary drawings of machines, with each working part carefully marked and distinguished. Indeed, some 18th-century philosophers viewed human beings as another kind of machine.*

detail. Other entries discussed medicine, as well as the use of dissection to discover the functions and parts of the body. Precise illustrations of human anatomy were also included, as were entries on astronomy, chemistry, and electricity. The authors of the *Encyclopédie* were also eager to discuss issues of constitutional government and political and religious authority. Five more volumes and a two-volume index were added by 1780.

Because of its subtle attacks on organized religion, on religious miracles, and on the government of France in general, government officials banned the *Encyclopédie* throughout the country. But no matter how hard it tried, the government could not stop printers from printing the work. In all, 5,000 copies—an enormous number for a scholarly work—were run. The people held, in their own hands, a work that showed them the weaknesses, flaws, and corruption in their government and in their church. Its pages prepared the people for revolution.

The editors of the Encyclopédie *provided illustrations of hundreds of examples of rural industry, including cheesemaking. The room is full of cheesemaking implements, and the man on the stool is forcing the watery part (the whey) out of the cheese.*

CHAPTER 9

RISING STARS
WOMEN IN THE ENLIGHTENMENT

The Herschel household overflowed with music. In the mid-18th century, Caroline Herschel (or Lina, as she was affectionately called by her big brothers) toddled through their modest home in Germany listening to her father practice his oboe. He was a musician for the Prussian army, and as if it were a gift you could wrap up and offer, he gave his four sons and two daughters a love for music. When Caroline was three and came down with smallpox, the music soothed her gentle spirit, but the disease scarred her face and disfigured her left eye.

Although Caroline Herschel's father had never been formally educated, he wanted a good education for his children. But his wife had different ideas. She thought an education was a waste of time. Reluctantly, she allowed the boys to learn a bit of math and French along with the music, but when it came to the girls, she put her foot down. There were plenty of chores that needed to be done. The girls had no time for such nonsense as learning.

In true Cinderella fashion, Caroline spent all her waking hours working as a maid for the family. But whenever he could, her father would sneak Caroline away for short lessons. One clear frosty night Caroline and her father watched a comet, and he taught her the names of several constellations.

When Caroline was 10, she got seriously sick again, this time from typhus, a disease carried by rats and transferred to humans by fleas. The disease stunted Caroline's growth. She never grew taller than 4 feet 3 inches. Her

The astronomer and "comet hunter" Caroline Herschel sits at a table recording astronomical observations called out by her brother, William, who used his large telescope to discover the planet Uranus. The Herschels had a fruitful scientific partnership that enabled Caroline to make many astronomical discoveries herself.

Working together, William and Caroline Herschel constructed large telescopes such as this 20-foot model. These telescopes allowed them to look farther into space than anyone else had before. The eyepiece of the telescope is mounted at the top and was viewed from a platform that could be lowered and raised.

father told her that between the damage the smallpox had done and the damage from the typhus, no man would ever want to marry her. She was doomed to the life of a servant. But her favorite brother William had plans to rescue his sweet-natured sister, Lina, from a life of drudgery. He had moved to the British resort town of Bath, where he was working as a musician, and when Caroline Herschel turned 22, he brought her to live with him.

As he and Caroline traveled through the Netherlands, William pointed out the constellations, just as her father had done when she was a child. And when they stopped in London before heading to Bath, William dragged his sister from optical shop to optical shop to look at lenses. William Herschel had a hobby that was soon to become a full-time occupation—astronomy.

William Herschel's passion for peering deeper and deeper into space led him to make his own telescopes. He preferred the sharper images shown by reflecting telescopes, which used mirrors, over those of refracting telescopes, which bent light through curved lenses. It was not long before his reputation for building quality telescopes spread. Caroline Herschel helped her brother with his business. She spent long hours grinding and polishing mirrors for the reflecting telescopes that they not only sold, but also used for their own observations of the stars. William's obsession with astronomy filled their every spare moment, sometimes to such extremes that they did not take the time to eat or change their clothes. In her writings, Caroline described feeding her brother bits of food as he worked on the same project for 16 hours straight.

Caroline complained that every room in the Herschels' home had been turned into a telescope workshop. They experimented with the sort of refracting telescopes that Galileo had made in the early 1600s; and they experimented with the reflecting telescopes that Isaac Newton had made in the mid-1600s. They made small telescopes and they made large telescopes. One was so enormous that the Herschels could actually walk through it. To hold it pointing toward the sky, they built scaffolding to support the tube. Long wooden ladders leaned against an observation platform near the top. The whole structure was mounted on a base that rotated so that they could point the telescope in any direction. William and Caroline communicated to assistants on the ground through a speaking tube. The assistants' job was to turn the base. The rickety scaffolding was dangerous, and more than once the whole thing almost collapsed on them. The telescope was so cumbersome and difficult to maneuver that the Herschels eventually destroyed it and returned to using their smaller and more manageable telescopes.

By this time, Caroline had caught William's astronomy bug. At night she spent time with him observing the sky, and during the day she performed the complicated mathematical calculations that plotted their observations. Even though Caroline had mastered the necessary algebra, geometry, and trigonometry, she never learned the multiplication tables. She used to keep a "cheat sheet" nearby to use while working with her data.

When William left on his frequent business trips, Caroline spent the evenings peering through her own telescope, making methodical sweeps of the skies searching for comets. In 1783 she noticed hazy clouds in the sky. She realized she had discovered three new nebulae—the material that forms stars. In 1786 she discovered her first comet. She wrote to several astronomers about her find, and soon many were calling it the "first lady's comet" because it was the first comet to be found by a woman. King George III recognized Caroline Herschel's abilities and provided her with a yearly salary so that she could continue her work as William's assistant. The salary may not have been much, but it was a giant sum in terms of recognition.

In 1797 Caroline Herschel found seven more comets—that made eight comets in all, six of which now bear her name. She also dug into a new project—adding to and correcting the catalogue of stars then used by astronomers. Her new index to the stars included hundreds of stars that the previous author had left out. In 1798 she submitted it to the Royal Society, the British national academy of science. For

On this page from Caroline Herschel's journal of August 1786, she writes of a star appearing out of focus at the center while another body, which turns out to be a comet, appears more sharply and moves in the direction of the star. Herschel discovered several comets, heavenly objects whose solid core is surrounded by gases and ice, forming a long tail. Their appearance in the sky is often unexpected.

"Decency, which was due principally to the women who gathered society in their homes, made minds more agreeable, and reading made them more solid in the long run."

—Voltaire, *The Age of Louis XIV*, 1751

all her efforts in astronomy, Caroline Herschel received many awards, including an honorary membership in the Royal Society—an honor in science that today would be considered second only to the Nobel Prize.

Despite her deformities and her early life of thankless labor, Caroline Herschel never lost her enchanting spirit. The world's most important scientists and mathematicians often came calling for an evening of conversation and star gazing with her. Even at the age of 83, the spry Herschel was still keeping the late hours of an astronomer. Her nephew wrote of her, "She runs about the town with me, and skips up her two flights of stairs. In the morning, till eleven or twelve, she is dull and weary, but as the day advances she gains life, and is quite 'fresh and funny' at ten p.m., and sings old rhymes, nay, even dances." On her 96th birthday, she received a letter from the King of Prussia, Frederick William IV, announcing that she was to receive the Gold Medal for science.

Caroline Herschel received medals and memberships, awards and accolades, yet perhaps the most fitting memorials are the comets and asteroid named after her.

A WOMAN'S PLACE IS IN THE——SALON?

Long before Caroline Herschel redefined the heavens, European women had begun to redefine their roles. In the early 17th century, outstanding women were becoming active on the social and intellectual scene. Some of these women, often with aristocratic backgrounds, were able to get an education, and this allowed them to participate in the intellectual life of

The salon hostesses of Paris invited writers, artists, and musicians to join them and present their works. In this painting, English tea is served in the Salon of the Four Mirrors at a Paris home in 1764 as the 8-year-old prodigy Wolfgang Amadeus Mozart plays the clavichord, a pianolike instrument.

their countries. They attended lectures of scientists and literary figures. They wrote essays and poems. They corresponded with royalty, philosophers, and scientists. Some made their mark by hosting "salons" that were attended by the leading philosophers and intellectuals of Europe.

Technically, a "salon" is a large room for receiving and entertaining guests. But in the 18th century, the meaning of this term shifted. It came to mean not just a place to meet, but the meetings themselves. These regular meetings consisted of intellectuals—small groups of people, sitting around a fire daring to think outside the traditional boundaries. Salons evolved during the Enlightenment from the literary salons of the 1730s, to the philosophical salons of the 1760s, to the political salons in the 1780s, growing and changing along with the interests of the participants. In England these informal circles were more likely to be called "conversation parties." But no matter what the current topic was or where in Europe these gatherings took place, intelligent, competent women organized and ran these fashionable meetings.

Dénis Diderot, the editor of the *Encyclopédie,* said of the women who ran the salons, "Women accustom us to discuss with charm and clearness the driest and thorniest of subjects. We talk to them unceasingly; we wish them to listen; we are afraid of tiring or boring them." Salon hostesses decided who would be invited and what topics would be discussed. They controlled the tone of the discussions, encouraging opposing ideas while preventing the discussions from sinking into foul language or overheated arguments. The hostesses also made sure that everyone spoke in straightforward language so that all those present could understand the speakers. Guests were often from different fields—a mix of artists, musicians, scientists, philosophers, writers, and other intellectuals. Clear explanations in laymen's terms were important so that everyone could be involved in the discussions. The salon was not a place for idle gossip. New ideas were exchanged. Controversial plays were performed away from the critical eye of the censor. Music recitals, painting exhibitions, poetry readings, demonstrations of new inventions— all entertained the guests. Salons attracted the greatest thinkers of the time.

In France, Madame Anne Thérèse de Lambert was one of the outstanding hostesses of the early 18th century. Born in 1647, de Lambert had been encouraged by her stepfather to read and become educated. She married a captain in the French Royal Regiment. But when he was killed, she was left a widow with a daughter.

De Lambert's concern for the education of the young led her to write two books of advice, one for her daughter and one for her son. "Nothing is so badly appreciated," she wrote in the book for her daughter, "as the education given to young women: all that is expected of them is that they should be attractive to men." Madame de Lambert's progressive opinions

"*L*et not men then in the pride of power, use the same arguments that tyrannic kings and venal ministers have used, and fallaciously assert that woman ought to be subjected because she has always been so."

—Mary Wollstonecraft, *A Vindication of the Rights of Woman,* 1792

about the education of women stood in stark contrast to those of the French philosopher and writer Jean-Jacques Rousseau. Although Rousseau shared the "new" idea that young girls from well-to-do families should be educated at home instead of being packed up and sent off to a convent, he felt their education should be limited to skills they could use at home. He wrote, "[girls] should be educated at home, by their mothers; they should learn all the arts of the home from cooking to embroidery."

Rousseau was strongly opposed to this new trend of women participating in intellectual debate. He felt they had no place in the world of science, politics, or philosophy. He certainly did not believe they should host the leading *male* intellectuals of the time in their salons. This is all the more surprising given the opening line of his most famous work, *The Social Contract,* "Man is born free but everywhere is in chains." In fact, Rousseau spent most of his life wrestling with the problem presented in that first line.

Women were casting off chains of their own. They were enjoying their exposure to the exciting new ideas of the Enlightenment far too much to be stopped by Rousseau or anyone else. In 1710, Madame de Lambert, at the age of 63, opened a salon in Paris, and her career as a hostess began in earnest. Two nights a week for the next 23 years, she received scholars, writers, and artists. Madame de Lambert's rules were very strict. Everyone was required to be polite, and show good manners and respect toward one another. She cultivated serious discussions in literature, science, and philosophy. On Tuesdays she hosted writers, artists, and intellectuals. On Wednesdays society people were invited to her home. Madame de Lambert made a great many social and political connections over the years and through her influence several philosophers were elected to the prestigious French Academy of Sciences, which was (and is) a great honor. Academy members are elected to life terms, and the distinction often caps a long and distinguished career in arts and letters.

Another hostess who welcomed the brightest minds of the day into her home was Marie Thérèse Geoffrin. Had

This portrait of Madame Marie Thérèse Geoffrin, who died in 1777, was painted in 1840, suggesting that her reputation as a salon hostess continued well into the next century. Geoffrin entertained a large circle of French philosophers, as well as English scholars such as David Hume.

Geoffrin chosen to follow tradition, her wealth could have guaranteed her a life of idle pastimes. But Geoffrin was not interested in spending her days overseeing servants and dabbling in "accepted" activities. After her husband died in 1750, she opened her salon in Paris.

Strong-willed and disciplined, Madame Geoffrin soon had a loyal following of guests who loved and admired her for her common sense and generosity. She put a great deal of thought into her guest lists in order to create the right atmosphere for lively and stimulating discussions. She was not ashamed to admit that her entire education came from those evenings in her salon. Even though her education was more limited than other hostesses of the time, her salon grew to be truly cosmopolitan. Writers and philosophers from several European countries gathered at her feet. Her salon was called "the salon of the *Encyclopédie*" because

Voltaire gives the first reading of one of his plays, The Orphan of China, *in Madame Geoffrin's salon. The drama was based on a Chinese novel brought to Europe and translated into French by a Jesuit missionary in the 1740s. Voltaire and other Enlightenment thinkers were fascinated by Chinese culture.*

"Women fill the intervals of conversation and of life, like the padding that one inserts in cases of china; they are valued at nothing, and [yet] everything breaks without them."

—Salon hostess Suzanne Necker, on women's role in the salons, letter to Baron Friedrich von Grimm, 1777

many of the contributors to the French encyclopedia met there. Madame Geoffrin herself made generous financial contributions to the project.

MARY, MARY, QUITE CONTRARY

Mary Wollstonecraft had lost count of her family's moves across England and Wales. Why couldn't her father succeed at being a gentleman farmer? How many times would he have to fail and move again before he would give up? If only he wouldn't drink so much. Mary's home life had never been happy. Her brother, the favorite, was insensitive to his sisters. Mary could hardly wait to get away from home.

After finishing her self-education by reading and reading and reading even more, Wollstonecraft tried working as a companion to a rich woman, as head of a girls' boarding-school, and as a teacher. None of these made her any happier. But when she published *Thoughts on the Education of Girls* in 1787, Wollstonecraft realized she had found something that did make her happy—writing.

Not surprisingly, in this book Wollstonecraft made the point that the goal of women's education should be to make them independent. Independent women did not have to stay in unhappy homes. They could make their own happiness. Women out on their own were a part of the world. Wollstonecraft argued that all human beings have a right to do what makes them happy. She complained, "How many women thus waste life away the prey of discontent, who might have practiced as physicians, regulated a farm, managed a shop, and stood erect, supported by their own industry, instead of hanging their heads surcharged with the dew of sensibility, that consumes the beauty to which it at first gave lustre."

Wollstonecraft discovered she had ideas, passions, and opinions about matters that had nothing to do with house and home. She wrote an essay called *A Vindication of the Rights of Man* in which she stood up for the principles of the French Revolution of 1789. In part she was reacting to the politicians who were against change. Many political leaders argued that it was important to keep traditional customs and warned against revolutionary actions. Did this mean keeping women in their place? It was clear to Wollstonecraft that all human beings possessed the power to think rationally, to make decisions for themselves. It was not something that belonged only to the monarchy, the church—or men in general, for that matter.

Wollstonecraft believed that all human beings had the right to make informed political decisions—and that some of those decisions might just be revolutionary. And it followed that if human beings could make their own political choices, democracy would be the preferred form of government rather than monarchy and despotism. By defending a

Mary Wollestonecraft was a serious writer and thinker who faced the issues of her time, including women's rights, head on. Her husband, William Godwin, wrote, "Her feelings had a character of peculiar strength and decision."

Teach the Girls

66 **HANNAH MORE, STRICTURES ON THE MODERN SYSTEM OF FEMALE EDUCATION, 1799**

Hannah More was a member of the British equivalent of the salon, known as the Bluestocking Circle. The members rejected the aristocracy's ideal life, composed of endless pleasure and primping. In fact, the group's name comes from blue wool stockings that were not up to the standard of black silk stockings that the well-to-do wore with evening dress.

Like many other woman writers participating in the Enlightenment during the 18th century, Hannah More wrote several books and essays about the lack of a rounded female education. In Strictures on the Modern System of Female Education, *published in 1799, she called for radical reform of the educational opportunities available to girls and young women.*

The profession of ladies, to which the bent of their instruction should be turned, is that of daughters, wives, mothers and mistresses of families. They should be therefore trained with a view to these several conditions and be furnished with a stock of ideas, and principles, and qualifications, and habits ready to be applied and appropriated, as occasion may demand, to each of these respective situations: for though the arts which merely embellish life must claim admiration; yet when a man of sense comes to marry, it is a companion whom he wants, and not an artist. It is not merely a creature who can paint, and play, and dress and dance; it is a being who can comfort and counsel him; one who can reason, and reflect, and feel, and judge, and act, and discourse, and discriminate; one who can assist him in his affairs, lighten his cares, soothe his sorrows, purify his joys, strengthen his principles, and educate his children.

The chief end to be proposed in cultivating the understanding of women, is to qualify them for the practical purposes of life...A lady studies, not that she may qualify herself to become an orator or a pleader; not that she may learn to debate, but to act. She is to read the best books, not so much to enable her to talk of them, as to bring the improvements which they furnish, to the rectification of her principles, and the formation of her habits. The great uses of study are to enable her to regulate her own mind, and to be useful to others.

person's right to use reason and rationality, Wollstonecraft put herself in the forefront of the Enlightenment.

When Wollstonecraft further examined women's role in society, she realized she was not alone in her discontent. In 1792 she wrote a public letter, much like a long version of today's letters to the editor in the newspaper, called *Vindication of the Rights of Woman*. She argued in it that the current situation hurt everyone, not just women: "Would men but generously snap our chains and be content with rational fellowship instead of slavish obedience, they would find us more observant daughters, more affectionate sisters, more faithful wives, and more reasonable mothers—in a word better citizens."

Mary Wollestonecraft's A Vindication of the Rights of Woman, published in 1792, championed women's equality with men. This copy of the book demonstrates its huge influence on the women's rights movement— it was inscribed by its owner, the 19th-century American leader of the movement for women's right to vote, Susan B. Anthony.

"If I exert my talents in writing I may support myself in a comfortable way. I am then going to be the first of a new genus."
—Mary Wollstonecraft, letter to her sister Everina, November 7, 1787

Throughout her life Mary Wollstonecraft wrote about women's struggles. Her own life was cut short from complications from childbirth when she was only 38. Her daughter, whom she would know for only 10 days, would grow up to be an author and commentator on the ills of society, too. Mary Wollstonecraft Shelley wrote the novel *Frankenstein*.

Women happily became the rising stars in public affairs and literary life. The belief that natural rights and equality should be granted universally to men and women awakened the first stirrings of feminist writers. Active women identified education—at home, in schools, and in salons—as the way for their gender to advance in the world. The salons and conversation groups hosted by women provided a safe place where philosophers and writers could exchange ideas in an atmosphere of respect and harmony. With the clever guidance of women across Europe, the new ideas of the Enlightenment spread.

This 1774 British cartoon mocks the patriotic women of Edenton, North Carolina, who held a "tea party" to express their sympathy for the Bostonians who protested taxes on tea by throwing cartons of British tea off a ship into Boston Harbor. The women are signing a petition objecting to the purchase of British tea.

CHAPTER 10

HEADS ROLLING
DEMOCRACY AND THE CONSENT OF THE PEOPLE

On August 29, 1618, Hugo Grotius nodded to the doorkeeper at the Hague, in Holland. Was he late for the meeting? The doorkeeper told him that Barnevelt, a fellow Dutch statesman, had already arrived and pointed toward the stairs. Grotius went up. But when he opened the door to the meeting room, a guard grabbed Grotius. Barnevelt had already been seized. The two were pushed out of the room. What was happening?

Grotius and Barnevelt watched, confused, as their accusers served as judges. Barnevelt's trial was brief, and the verdict swift—Off with his head! Then the inquisitors turned to Grotius: What say you? Grotius refused to ask for a pardon. It was the same as admitting guilt. He had done nothing wrong. He would *not* say that he had—even if it meant losing his head. He wrote a long letter to his wife, telling her that he trusted in God. He prayed. But he had little hope. His head would roll just as surely as Barnevelt's had.

Grotius was dragged into court. His accusers presented no written charges. They did not allow him a defense lawyer. They gave Grotius a single sheet of paper to make notes for his defense, but no time to prepare it. Again, the verdict was guilty, but they must have taken pity on Grotius—they sentenced him to life in prison. A shocked and confused Grotius was dragged off and locked away. He was 36 years old.

How did this happen? What *were* the charges? It would be a whole year before Grotius would even find out what he had been charged with—high treason. And for what? Just because he was trying to get the two religious factions dividing Holland to live peaceably with one another? Surely they could see how devoted he was to his country?

Grotius had a lot of time in prison to think about his life. A child prodigy, he had mastered Latin before he was 8,

This portrait of Hugo Grotius was painted long after his stay in prison. A deeply religious man, he wears the starched, ruffled collar often worn by Puritans in England and Calvinists in the Netherlands, who followed the teachings of John Calvin.

"*T*he natural liberty of man is to be free from any superior power on earth, and not to be under the will or legislative authority of man, but to have only the law of nature for his rule."

—John Locke, *Two Treatises of Government*, 1690

gone to university at 11, and graduated from law school when he was 16. He had written plays, poems, histories, and legal documents. He was a scholar and a lawyer, not a criminal. He had been attorney general for the Netherlands, served in its legislature—how could they throw him in prison?

At least his jailers let him have his books. And his wife, Marie, and their children could come and go and share his two rooms. Marie was a proud, strong woman. She had refused the tiny allowance the government had offered for food in prison. She would take care of him. She would take care of all of them. She arranged for Grotius's books to be delivered to him in prison. They came in a 4-foot-long chest. When he had pored through the chest's contents, he sent them back and a new batch was delivered. The chest passed the guards so many times they stopped examining it. Marie noticed how careless the guards had become, and she thought of a plan to exploit the situation to her husband's benefit.

One morning, Grotius prayed for an hour. When he was finished, he stood, carefully spread his clothes on a chair by his bed, and, in his underwear, climbed into the book chest. It was a tight fit, and the only air he would get came through the keyhole, but he would rather die attempting to escape then spend his life confined. Marie called to the guards. Would they please carry away the books? She worried her husband was ruining his health spending so much time with his nose in their pages. The guards looked at Grotius's clothes on the chair and the pulled bed curtains and assumed he was asleep.

Marie's maid left Holland by boat, keeping a close watch on the chest. While leading the men she had paid to unload the chest and carry it ashore, there was a very close call. The men nearly dropped the chest in fear when they felt something alive moving in it. The quick-witted maid laughed and told the workmen the books were indeed full of life and spirit. When she was at last alone and away from spying eyes, the maid released Grotius, who disguised himself as a bricklayer and fled for Paris, where he was to meet Marie.

Grotius found himself in the midst of the Thirty Years' War that had been raging across Europe since 1618. The religious disputes between Protestants and Catholics favored no nationality. Everyone fought—from France to Spain to Germany and beyond. No matter where he looked, Grotius saw cruelty. The barbarian behavior he was witnessing upset him so much that he published a book, *The Laws of War and Peace,* in protest in 1625. He explained in the preface, "I saw in the whole Christian world a license [for] fighting at which even barbarous nations might blush. Wars were begun on trifling pretexts or none at all, carried on without any reference to law, divine or human."

To solve the problem of religious and political warfare, Grotius believed he needed to define a clear standard of international conduct. There must be a way for nations to behave with human decency. He believed that if opposing sides could agree to a set of universal principles, it would regulate them and bind them together. In *The Laws of War and Peace,* Grotius set out to uncover those principles, or "natural laws," as he called them. Natural laws must be common to all human societies. For him it did not matter what religious or political commitments people had; they could still join hands by embracing natural laws, which were consistent with the laws of God. "Natural law," he wrote, "is so unalterable that it cannot be changed by God himself." Grotius believed these universal standards of human conduct could be found by reason. And who was better suited to figure them out than a onetime child prodigy?

Grotius understood that universal principles ought to govern the behavior of all states, including the behavior of those at war with each other on land and on the high seas. Countries would need to

The title page of Hugo Grotius's book The Laws of War and Peace, *one of the most original texts on international law, presents readers with a choice: justice and peace, represented by the figure at the left, holding a dove; or war, represented by the soldier on the right. Grotius believed that war was sometimes justified, but the bloody battle scene at the bottom warns of its consequences.*

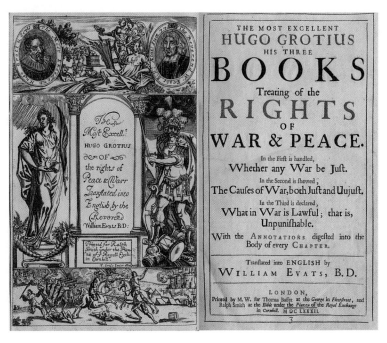

pledge to abide by the international rules. He believed that this was especially important for those who saw people whose religious beliefs were different from their own as enemies.

Grotius realized there should be a legal category that could be called "the rights of war," legal duties that apply especially during times of military conflict. Their purpose would be to limit destructive human behavior. Grotius argued that there are procedures to resolve international issues of war and peace, as follows: Warring parties should meet and try to work out their problems, even while they are at war. They should learn to trust each other and to make binding agreements. They should work to achieve compromises. Through negotiation, each party gains something while giving up something in return. And if the par-

During the Thirty Years' War, the German city of Magdeburg was the site of a fierce battle. The Swedish king Gustavus Adolphus, fighting on the Protestant side, seized the city, and when the German Catholic Count Tilly and his army counterattacked in May 1631, the Swedes set the whole city ablaze.

> *"Reason…teaches all mankind who will but consult it that, being all equal and independent, no one ought to harm another in his life, health, liberty, or possessions."*
>
> —John Locke, *Two Treatises of Government*, 1690

ties are deadlocked in their negotiations, they should either engage in single combat, one person standing for all the others, or draw lots to determine the winner.

One of the most lasting concepts that Grotius developed was that of a "just war." According to Grotius, there were only three valid reasons for entering a war. The first was the need for defense against an actual or immediate threat of injury. The second was the need to take action in order to recover what was legally due, such as lost territory or monetary payments that had been promised. The third was the need to take action as punishment for an actual injury suffered. Only these legally defined conditions could justify going to war.

There were many different opinions about what Grotius had to say in *The Laws of War and Peace*. The Catholic Church immediately placed it on its banned book list (where it remained for more than 275 years, until 1901). Others were not sure what to make of *rules* of war. But the king Gustav Adolphus of Sweden admired Grotius's idea of principles that humanity would follow even in times of extreme conflict. When the king died in 1632, a copy of Grotius's book was found in the tent the king had used as headquarters while traveling. With *The Laws of War and Peace* was a document with the king's command to hire Grotius as a Swedish ambassador.

HEADLESS

On January 30, 1649, Charles I, king of England, stepped out of the palace into the bitter cold. He was flanked on both sides by soldiers who escorted him to the scaffold. King Charles had dressed carefully that morning, his last morning.

Spectators from all walks of life witnessed the beheading of King Charles I of England in 1649. At the far right, one lady faints from the shock of the sight.

Oliver Cromwell's army of Puritan reformers had been engaged in a civil war throughout the 1640s, and he seized power in England soon after the king was beheaded.

He had worn an extra shirt against the cold. He would not allow the cold to make him shiver and let his enemies later claim he shook from fear. He would not give them the satisfaction. King Charles walked briskly toward his own death.

The king had expected to speak to the crowd before he lost his head. But rows of soldiers held the people back, keeping them far from the king. So instead, he read his last speech to the handful of men nearby. When he finished, he handed his prayer book to the bishop, instructing him to "remember." Then he gathered his hair and tucked it under a white cap. He wanted nothing to slow the executioner's axe. When the people in the crowd saw the arc of the axe falling and heard the thud as it hit the block, they moaned in unison. And when the assistant executioner held up the severed head, no one cheered. Their king was dead.

Had Charles's willfulness brought this on? King Charles had never seen eye to eye with Parliament. When Parliament held back money, Charles closed it down. When it refused to impose the taxes he needed, he closed it down again. Finally, Charles decided he would rule without a parliament at all, closing it down permanently. For 11 years Charles ruled

alone. Every morning, even on hunting days, Charles prayed.
He was true to his faith—he believed in the teachings of the
Church of England. And Charles wanted Scotland to be
true to his faith as well. But the Scots had different ideas,
and they fought to protect them. And they won.

Not only were these wars ultimately a losing cause—
they depleted the national treasury. Charles needed more
money to run the country after the wars were over, so he
called a session of Parliament to help him raise it. Then the
king ordered it closed again. This time, however, Parliament
would not allow itself to be shut down. When Charles tried
to arrest its members, the militia protected them. Charles
found himself with a civil war on his hands.

The rebel leader, Oliver Cromwell, and his Roundheads
proved impossible for Charles to defeat. The Roundheads got
their name from the short haircuts they sported in defiance of
Charles and his wigged nobility. They were not members
of the Church of England; they were Puritans, who followed

*The death warrant for the execution
of Charles I was issued by a High
Court established by a vote of
Parliament. Although the king
claimed that the court did not have
the power to try him, the court signed
the warrant after a four-day trial.*

a strict religious discipline and wanted to simplify church ceremonies. And they wanted King Charles's head.

Parliament was loath to execute a king, even one that had been its sworn enemy for so long. Cromwell pushed for the death sentence, however, and he finally browbeat the reluctant members into signing his order of execution. Charles's fate was sealed.

WORDS TO DIE BY

Inscribed on the English philosopher John Locke's tombstone are the words, "Stop Traveler! Near this place lieth John Locke. If you ask what kind of a man he was, he answers that he lived content with his own small fortune. Bred a scholar, he made his learning subservient only to the cause of truth. This thou will learn from his writings, which will show thee everything else concerning him." It is indeed through John Locke's writings that we understand the man and, along with him, the times in which he lived.

In his *Two Treatises of Government,* published in 1690, Locke opposed the idea that rulers, whether in England, France, or elsewhere in Europe, held their positions by virtue of God's command. Locke argued that all men are free. They are at liberty to do as they wish as long as they do not harm others. They are free to own property and to pursue happiness. If people came together, to cooperate and work together, then most people would be better off. They would be protected by the group they created working as one. Although this would mean that they would have to give up certain liberties in exchange for benefits for everyone, it was a better life. According to Locke, writing in *Two Treatises,* "The only way whereby any one divests himself of his natural liberty, and puts on the bonds of Civil Society is by agreeing with other men to join and unite into a community, for their comfortable, safe, and peaceable living one among another, in a secure enjoyment of their properties." The question for Locke was how much freedom people had to give up when joining together.

One freedom Locke believed should never be sacrificed was the freedom of religious belief. Locke wrote a moving

> "*To* understand political power right, and derive it from its original, we must consider what state all men are naturally in, and that is a state of perfect freedom to order their action and dispose of their possessions and persons as they think fit, within the bounds of the law of nature, without asking leave, or depending upon the will of any other man."
>
> —John Locke, *Two Treatises of Government,* 1690

letter that explained why he thought it was wrong for any group to attempt to force its religious beliefs on another. According to Locke, religion is an inner belief that cannot be coerced. His *Letters Concerning Toleration* had been published in 1689 and had a major impact on thinkers all across Europe, as well as in America.

According to Locke, "liberty of conscience is every man's natural right." He meant that people should be able to choose their own religious belief. A ruler does not have the right to choose it for them. It followed naturally that civil authorities should have no control over one's religious life. In Locke's words, "the care of souls does not belong to the magistrate," and "nobody ought to be compelled in matters of religion either by force or law."

Such ideas inspired the framers of the U.S. Constitution almost a century later. The First Amendment to the Constitution reads, "Congress shall make no law respecting an establishment of religion, or prohibiting the free exercise thereof." The language of the amendment prevents any part of the government from setting up a church. It prevents it from passing laws that aid religions, or from giving preference to one religion. And it prevents it from forcing belief or disbelief in any religion. By incorporating this amendment into the Constitution, the United States avoided a great many religious conflicts. It is the basis of the separation of church and state, a key constitutional principle.

Locke's theories are the foundation of modern democratic and constitutional government. One of Locke's principles is the idea that people live together in a political union established by their own consent. If the government is not based on the consent of the majority of the people, then the political leaders have unlawfully taken control. This was the idea behind the U.S. Declaration of Independence, written in 1776. The American revolutionaries claimed that their rights had been violated by the king of England, George III. Therefore, they wrote, "whenever any form of Government becomes destructive of... Life, Liberty and the Pursuit of

IOHN LOCKE

In his Letters Concerning Toleration, *the English philosopher John Locke argued for constitutional government and religious tolerance. This edition portrayed Locke surrounded by a wreath of laurels. That symbol of honor linked him with the great philosophers, statesmen, and poets of the past.*

continues on page 152

A Glorious Revolution

" **THE ENGLISH DECLARATION OF RIGHTS, 1689**

In 1215 a group of English barons forced King John to sign a "Great Charter," or the Magna Carta. This was a great moment, proving for the first time that the power of the king could be limited by a written agreement. This charter granted Englishmen a number of rights, foremost among them the promise that "no freeman shall be captured or imprisoned…except by lawful judgment of his peers or by the law of the land."

Later monarchs failed to honor the principles of the Magna Carta. When violations of citizens' rights by King James II occurred in 1688, a citizen army opposing him was formed. The King fled, and Parliament decided that he had forfeited his claim to be king. Opposition leaders installed William, the Dutch prince of Orange, and his wife Mary, on the the throne instead. In order to be accepted as King William III, William had to accept the Declaration of Rights. This great event has been called the "Glorious Revolution" because it established the major principles of constitutional government. The monarch was installed by Parliament, the representatives of the people, rather than by God. These principles were also a major historical foundation for the U.S. Constitution, written in 1787, and also influenced French revolutionaries in 1789.

[1.] That the pretended power of suspending of Lawes or the execution of Lawes by Regall Authority without Consent of Parliament is illegall.

[2.] That the pretended power of dispensing with lawes or the Execution of lawes by regall authority as it has been assumed and exercised of late is illegall…

[4.] That levying of money for or to the use of the Crowne by pretence of Prerogative without Grant of Parliament for longer time or in other manner, than the same is or shall be granted is illegall.

[5.] That it is the right of the Subjects to petition the King and all Commitments and prosecutions for such petitioning are illegall.

[6.] That the raiseing or keeping a Standing Army within the Kingdom in time of Peace unlesse it be with consent of Parliament is against Law.

[7.] That the Subjects which are Protestants may have Armes for their defence Suitable to their Condition and as allowed by Law.

[8.] That Elections of Members of Parliament ought to be free.

[9.] That the freedome of Speech and debates or proceedings in Parliament ought not to be impeached or questioned in any Courte or place out of Parliament.

[10.] That excessive Bayle ought not to be required nor excessive fynes imposed nor cruel and unusuall Punishments inflicted.

[11.] That Jurors ought to be duely impannelled and returned and Jurors which passe upon men in tryalls for high Treason ought to be freeholders...

[13.] And that for redress of all grievances and for the amending, strengthening and preserving of the Lawes, Parliaments ought to be held frequently.

After King Charles II abandoned the throne in 1689, King William of Orange and Queen Mary became the new rulers of Britain. Wearing crowns and the king holding a scepter symbolizing royal authority, the new rulers are presented as supreme governors of England.

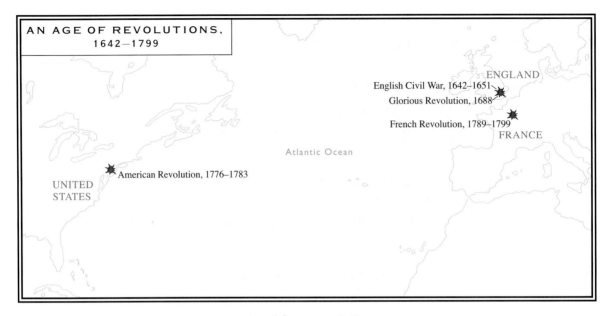

AN AGE OF REVOLUTIONS,
1642–1799

ENGLAND

English Civil War, 1642–1651
Glorious Revolution, 1688

French Revolution, 1789–1799

FRANCE

Atlantic Ocean

American Revolution, 1776–1783

UNITED
STATES

continued from page 149

Happiness... it is the right of the people to alter or abolish it, and to institute new Government." They proposed to create a new government "to secure these Rights." The American revolutionaries argued that such governments "[derive] their just powers from the Consent of the governed." In short, they put John Locke's political theory into action.

Locke's logical arguments undermined the legitimacy of all monarchies, for they were not based on the consent of the governed. Locke's *Treatises* on government stood as a justification for revolutionary movements in America and France, which put limits on the powers of kings and other rulers.

In America the position of king was replaced by the elected office of president, though there were some who wanted George Washington to assume the title of king. He refused. In this way Washington and the writers of the U.S. Constitution made sure that the highest office in the U.S. government would be held by an official elected by the people.

This illustration was created for a 1783 book on the history of England. The original caption read, "The Manner in which the American Colonies Declared themselves Independant of the King of England."

EPILOGUE
BENJAMIN FRANKLIN, ENLIGHTENED AMERICAN

Kant asked, "What is enlightenment?" Now you might ask, "What does the Enlightenment mean to me?" No doubt, Benjamin Franklin would be delighted to show you. Franklin was the 10th of 17 children. His father was a candlemaker, but because this was the Enlightenment, Franklin and his siblings no longer were destined to be candlemakers. At 16, Franklin was working for his older brother, a printer in Boston.

Franklin badly wanted to write for the newspaper his brother published, but his older brother would have none of it. So Franklin pretended to be someone else: a middle-aged widow named Silence Dogood. He slipped "her" essays under his brother's door at night. This completely fooled his brother, who printed them in the paper. The public loved them.

Older brothers do not always make the best bosses, so in 1723, at the age of 17, Franklin ran away. He arrived in Philadelphia with nothing but some change in his pocket and a few rolls to eat. But this was the Enlightenment, so starting out poor no longer meant being condemned to poverty forever. By the time Franklin turned 24, he owned his own print shop and had started a newspaper. He founded an organization called the Leather Apron Club, where ambitious tradespeople like himself met on Friday nights.

"*Learning, whether Speculative or Practical, is, in Popular or Mixt Governments, the Natural Source of Wealth and Honour.*"

—Benjamin Franklin, *Poor Richard's Almanack*, 1749

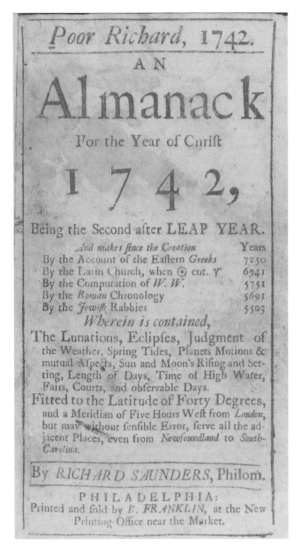

Benjamin Franklin's many writings include those that appeared under the byline "Poor Richard" in a yearly "almanack" of practical advice. Franklin used this publication to tell readers about important events and issues and to give such advice as "Beware of the young Doctor and the old Barber."

They brainstormed regarding all sorts of improvements for the city of Philadelphia—the first fire department, the first non-religious college, the first public library, you name it. Books—and the ideas in them—were no longer available only to the wealthy. It was the time of the Enlightenment. The Leather Apron Club meetings were not all work, though. Franklin and his friends loved to sing, and often they would sing well into the night.

Before long, Franklin was very wealthy. His newspaper was the *Washington Post* of its day. He franchised print shops up and down the coast. He was a self-made man of the Enlightenment. He donated money to all the churches in Philadelphia and contributed to the building of Philadelphia's first synagogue. Over time, the other members of the Leather Apron Club also grew into successful businesspeople.

Inspired by a suggestion to begin a society for learning, in 1743, Franklin wrote a pamphlet called "A Proposal for Promoting Useful Knowledge Among the British Plantations in America." He began by suggesting that "The first drudgery of settling new colonies, which confines the attention of people to mere necessaries, is now pretty well over." People now had the time to turn their attention toward science and the arts. On May 25, 1743, those casual Leather Apron Club evenings of singing into the early morning hours ended, and the American Philosophical Society held its first meeting.

That first year, its members studied "useful" sciences. They looked for ways to improve farming. They looked for ways to improve mining. They looked for ways to make better maps. They looked for ways to brew a better beer. But soon their interests expanded into all areas of science, and the society became a major engine advancing the ideas of the Enlightenment. New members joined one of six groups: Geography, Mathematics, Natural Philosophy (that is, physics) and Astronomy, Medicine and Anatomy, Natural History and Chemistry, Trade and Commerce, Mechanics and Architecture, Husbandry (the art of cultivating plants and animals), and American Improvements. Franklin's society still meets regularly today, making it the oldest scholarly society in the United States.

Franklin retired from the newspaper business at 42. He wanted more time to pursue the types of things he enjoyed discussing in society meetings, particularly inventions and politics. Franklin questioned everything, and his questions brought answers in the form of practical things that enhanced everyday life—a stove that heated houses efficiently, for instance, and bifocals (or "double spectacles" as he called them), which saved him from the chore of constantly switching back and forth between his distance glasses and his reading glasses.

But what Franklin is most remembered for is his work with electricity, particularly his experiments with lightning. Until Franklin's experiments people thought that thunder and lightning were acts of God—a very angry God. Franklin recognized lightning as static electricity on an *enormous* scale. The French had proved

Beginning in 1743, Benjamin Franklin carried out many experiments to understand the nature of electricity and how it is conducted by various materials. To aid his experiments with lightning, he constructed models of differently shaped buildings.

Electrical experimentation was all the rage in the 1740s among educated Europeans. A popular experiment involved producing static electricity by rubbing a glass rod with a silk cloth. In this demonstration the experimenter is holding an electrified glass rod above a boy's head who is suspended by silk threads. Because the boy is insulated by the silk, the electric charge passes from the glass rod onto the boy's head and jumps from his nose to the lady's finger when she brings it close, giving them both a mild shock.

this theory before Franklin's electrical experiments with kite and key, but Franklin found a practical application in the proof: the lightning rod. Before Franklin's lightning rod, whole towns burned to the ground from fires started by lightning, and many people were killed. Franklin's pointed lightning rod safely channeled the charge into the ground. Franklin never applied for a patent for his lightning rod, or for any of his many other inventions, for that matter. Even so, his manufacture and sale of lightning rods served him well by making him famous. Universities leaped at the chance to honor Franklin by bestowing honorary doctoral degrees upon him.

Franklin may have been amused at receiving all these accolades, because he never took himself too seriously and wouldn't have seen himself as a "doctor," but he did see himself as a loyal Englishman. So when Britain began taxing its American colonies heavily to recover the money it had spent fighting the French and Indian War, angering the colonists as a result, Franklin went to England to mediate the dispute. Like all good men of the Enlightenment, he believed that through reason, England and the colonies could resolve their problems.

But that did not happen. No one knows exactly how, but while he was in England, Franklin somehow got hold of letters that the royal governor of Massachusetts, Thomas Hutchinson, had written. In them, the governor revealed that he was not on the side of the people of Massachusetts, as he pretended to be, but was working to curtail their liberties. Franklin sent the letters to America and leaked them to the public. His plan was that the English king, George III, would be forced to recall the governor and replace him with someone more sympathetic to the colonists.

The plan backfired. The letters created a huge scandal. Franklin was summoned to appear before the English

Foreign Ministry, where the officials gave him a tongue lashing. He was treated like a delinquent. It was at that moment that Franklin realized that the English would always consider the colonists second-class citizens. Franklin entered that meeting as an Englishman, but he exited an American. He returned home, enlightened.

In 1776, the Second Continental Congress selected Franklin, along with four other delegates, to draft the Declaration of Independence. Thomas Jefferson did most of the writing, then gave his draft to Franklin to edit. In the second paragraph, Jefferson listed what enlightened thinkers believed to be "truths." Jefferson wrote, "We hold these truths to be *sacred.*" With a bold stroke of his pen, Franklin crossed out the word *sacred* and replaced it with *self-evident.*

In true Enlightenment form, Franklin shifted the origin of those "truths" from religious belief to individual reason. Individual human rights and basic freedoms were about to trump the long-held tradition of the divine right of kings. And Benjamin Franklin was leading the way. As one French baron put it, Franklin "snatched the lightning from the heavens, the scepter from the tyrants." The Enlightenment had spread from Europe to America. Now *revolution* would spread from America to Europe.

Paying for the revolution became Franklin's problem. His next task was to convince the king of France to bankroll America's fight for independence. How would Franklin convince a king who had no interest in American independence to pay for it? It was a daunting task, and a less-committed and visionary man might have failed. But Franklin did not shrink from the challenge.

"This is really a generous nation, fond of glory, and particularly that of protecting the oppressed."
—Benjamin Franklin on France, letter to Robert Livingston, March 4, 1782

On September 16, 1779, Benjamin Franklin wrote a promissory note to King Louis XVI of France, pledging that the new American government would repay the 3 million French livres that France agreed to lend the new nation. A livre was a monetary unit used in France at the time.

The jovial, newly appointed ambassador from the American colonies landed in Paris prepared to persuade King Louis XVI to join the American revolutionaries against the British. But the king refused to see him. So Franklin spent his evenings in the salons. He knew that it was in the salons that French politicians conducted business. There he exchanged ideas about liberty and equality. He argued the virtue of using reason not only in science but also in politics. While cultivating support for the American Revolution, he unintentionally also planted seeds for the French Revolution.

All the while, Franklin charmed his way into the hearts of the French people. Franklin rather ingeniously used his celebrity to wield influence on them. Just as rock stars and movie stars today are able to use their fame to raise money for their favorite causes, Franklin was able to leverage his "electric" personality. When Franklin

When Benjamin Franklin went to Paris to represent the rebelling American colonies, he sometimes wore a coonskin cap to emphasize his lack of aristocratic background. The people of Paris loved it.

arrived in France, he was greeted by frenzied fans. Merchants hawked Franklin ashtrays, Franklin knick-knacks—even Franklin wallpaper. Franklin created an image for himself of a simple backwoods Quaker to appeal to the French middle class—even though he didn't come from the backwoods and had never been a Quaker. He wore a coonskin hat. He wore woodsman's clothing. The French loved it. They thought all Americans must be moral, freedom-loving, peace-loving Quakers fighting against the tyranny of the king. Franklin never mentioned to them that this was not true.

The French king, aware of the people's growing discontent, could not afford to alienate them further. Perhaps he thought if he gave the beloved Franklin what he wanted, it would curry favor among the people. Or maybe Louis XVI was just hoping to get rid of Franklin—send him packing back to America and stop him from stirring up the middle class with his Enlightenment ideas. But in the end, he signed the check. Franklin got his money.

Benjamin Franklin used the salons of Paris to reach nobles and statesmen when King Louis XVI refused to see him. He discovered the great value of the salons and the women who hosted them: "I see that statesmen, philosophers, historians, poets, and men of learning of all sorts, are drawn around you, and seem as willing to attach themselves to you as straws about a fine piece of amber."

"I join with you most cor-
dially in rejoicing at the
return of peace. I hope it
will be lasting, and that
mankind will at length...
have reason enough to settle
their differences without
cutting throats; for, in my
opinion, there never was a
good war, or a bad peace."

—Benjamin Franklin, letter
to Sir Joseph Banks, president
of the Royal Society of
London, on the end of war
between England and the
American colonies,
July 27, 1783

Franklin returned to America a hero. His ideas, communicated with just the right words and wit, shaped the
new nation. Even the word *united* in the name "United States
of America" had come from Franklin's newspaper. Franklin
lived long enough to hear news of the French Revolution he
had inadvertently encouraged. He worried about the safety
of all the friends that he had made, but he supported the
French people in their struggle to obtain those "self-evident"
rights the French monarchy had denied them.

In his final years, he joined the abolitionist movement
against slavery. One of his last public acts was appealing to
Congress to abolish slavery (it failed). He did not live to see
the slave uprisings in San Domingue in 1791, in which
hundreds of thousands of slaves organized into a military
force that was eventually able to defeat the French armies in
control there. Then insurrection leaders established an
independent republic called Haiti, the first to be headed
by people of African descent. Although Franklin did not
believe that violence solved political problems, he would
have understood the longing for liberty that stirred the
Haitian Revolution.

Franklin died on April 17, 1790, at the age of 84. All the
clergy in Philadelphia—25 priests, ministers, and rabbis—
accompanied his casket to the grave. Franklin would have
agreed with Kant, that although he did not live in an
enlightened age, he lived in an age of enlightenment.

GLOSSARY

armada A fleet of warships

astrology The study of the supposed influence of the planets and stars, depending on their position in the universe, on humans and events

astronomy The study of objects, such as planets and stars, outside of the earth's atmosphere

axis The invisible line that runs through the north and south poles of the earth, on which the earth rotates

bifocals Eyeglasses which have two different kinds of lenses, one for correcting nearsightedness and one for correcting farsightedness

calculus A type of mathematics that includes rules for determining and examining motion, change, surface area, and other concepts

capillary The smallest size of blood vessel

cartography The science of mapmaking

caste A system of social classification in Hinduism that categorizes people based on their hereditary position in society; also, one of those social classes

chinoiserie (sheen-WAH-zer-EE) A style of porcelain, popular in the 17th century, that features a European version of Chinese designs and images

conquistador (con-KEE-stah-dor) A leader in the Spanish conquest of the Americas, especially of Mexico and Peru in the 16th century

despotism A system of government in which the ruler has unlimited and centralized power

devshirme (dehv-sheer-MEH) Ottoman sultans' system for recruiting non-Muslim boys to train as personal servants and soldiers, from the Turkish word meaning "harvest"

ellipse An oval

Enlightenment An intellectual movement in 18th-century Europe that fostered greater knowledge and progressive thinking, based on science and facts over religion and superstition

equator The invisible line encircling the earth that divides the earth in half and is directly perpendicular to its axis

exile To banish from one's home country, usually as punishment for a crime

factor A representative of a European trading company who conducted business in the so-called factories established by the company in the New World

Hafiz (hah-FEEZ) A person who knows the Quran so thoroughly that he can recite it from memory, with perfect pronunciation; word is derived from the Arabic for "to protect" or "to memorize"

heliocentrism In astronomical terms, having the sun at the center of the solar system, with all the planets revolving around it

hypothesis A theory or idea formulated in order to test and possibly prove its truth

indentured servant A person who travels to a new country by being sponsored by another person who pays the servant's passage and living expenses in return for work for a specific amount of time to repay the debt.

inoculation A method of preventing disease by deliberately inducing a mild form of the disease, resulting in future immunity to it

Inquisition An office of the Catholic Church charged with suppressing dissent and heretical ideas such as Copernicus's and Galileo's theory that the earth revolved around the sun

katib (kah-TEEB) A professional secretary in the Ottoman Empire

magistrate An official in China responsible for enforcing laws

malaria A disease transmitted by the bite of infected mosquitoes and characterized by high fever and chills.

mandarin A highly esteemed Chinese scholar

mausoleum A large building, usually made of stone, for entombing the dead aboveground

mercantilism An economic system in which nations attempted to increase their wealth through the acquisition of gold and trade with other countries

Mercator projection A method of drawing a map of the world so that the meridian lines, instead of being curved, are parallel; as a result, the circular globe is "projected" onto the flat surface in a more readable way

meridian An invisible north-south circle around the Earth that goes through the poles; also, the representation of this circle on a map through meridian lines

middle passage The second leg of the slave trade process, where slaves were crowded onto ships by European slave traders and transported to the New World for sale

minaret A tall tower of a mosque where summons for prayer are issued daily

missionary A person who works to convert others to a certain religion

monopoly Exclusive control of a certain industry or area in which there is no competition

mosque A building used for public worship by Muslims

muezzin (moo-EH-zeen) Person who calls others to prayer at a mosque

nebula A cloud of interstellar dust and gas that forms stars

paisley A fabric design characterized by the *boteh*, an Indian symbol of fertility; the design was adopted by the English in the 17th century

patent An official document granting a person the exclusive right to make, use, and sell his or her invention for a designated period of time

piston A moving part of an engine that produces power by sliding back and forth inside a cylinder

prism A glass object that splits light into various colors

quota A specific share or amount

Quran (kuh-RAN) The holy book of Islam, also spelled *Koran*

republic A form of government characterized by a head of state (usually a president) and a central governing body, both elected by the people

retrograde An astronomical term describing the movement of a celestial body in a backward motion opposite of its usual direction

rhombus A parallelogram with two pairs of parallel lines equal in length

rhumb A line on a mariner's compass that shows a constant track of a ship's bearing

salon A regular gathering of intellectuals for the purpose of discussing and learning about new ideas

sassafras A substance made of dried tree bark that 17th-century Europeans used for medicinal purposes

scaffold A platform upon which criminals are executed by hanging or beheading

shallop A small two-masted sailing ship

smallpox A contagious disease characterized by skin lesions, scarring, and pus

solar eclipse An astronomical event caused when the moon passes between the sun and the earth, temporarily blocking the sun from view

Torah A holy book of Judaism consisting of the first five books of the Hebrew bible

trading company A commercial organization (often sponsored by a government) to encourage and facilitate trade with other countries

typhus A bacterial disease characterized by high fever, delirium, rash, and stupor

yellow fever A serious contagious illness prevalent in warm-weather areas whose symptoms include high fever, yellowish coloring of the skin and body fluids, and sometimes bleeding

TIMELINE

1543
Publication of Nicolaus Copernicus's *On the Revolutions of the Heavenly Spheres,* announcing his theory of a heliocentric (sun-centered) system

1556–1605
Jalal al-Din Akbar rules India

1572–1620
Emperor Zhu Yizhun rules China

1588
Spanish Armada is defeated by the British navy

1600
British East India Company founded

1602
Captain Bartholomew Gosnold sets sail for the New World aboard the *Concord*

1605
Jahangir begins reign of Mughal India

1607
Jamestown, Virginia, first permanent English settlement in North America, is founded

1609
Galileo Galilei examines the orbits of Jupiter's moons by telescope

Johannes Kepler publishes *New Astronomy,* detailing his first two laws of planetary motion

1616
Galileo told by Catholic Church not to discuss his heliocentric ideas

1618–1648
Thirty Years' War

1619
First slave ship carrying Africans arrives in Virginia

1620
Pilgrims land in what is now Massachusetts; Plymouth Colony founded

1623
Dutch East India Company founded

1628
Shah Jahan begins his reign in Mughal India

William Harvey publishes *Anatomical Exercise on the Motion of the Heart and Blood in Animals,* describing how the blood circulates throughout the body

1631–1654
Taj Mahal built

1632
Galileo publishes *Dialogue Concerning the Two Chief World Systems,* defending the heliocentric view

1633
Galileo condemned by Inquisition, forced to renounce his belief in heliocentrism

1635
Shah Jahan ascends to the throne in Mughal India

1637
René Descartes publishes *Discourse on Method*

1642–1649
English Civil War

1649
Charles I of England beheaded; Oliver Cromwell, leader of the Roundheads, seizes power

1658
Aurangzeb becomes ruler of Mughal India

1660
Monarchy is restored in England

1667
Dutch cede New Netherland to the English

1687
Isaac Newton publishes *Mathematical Principles of Natural Philosophy*

1689
John Locke writes *Letters Concerning Toleration,* advocating religious tolerance

English "Glorious Revolution" produces the Declaration of Rights

1690
Locke publishes *Two Treatises of Government,* laying the foundation of modern democratic and constitutional government

1699
First English trading post in China

1712
The steam engine is developed in England

1717
Lady Mary Wortley Montagu publishes letter in England about smallpox inoculation used successfully in Turkey

1728
Jai Singh starts building observatories in India and builds city of Jaipur

1733
Voltaire publishes *Letters on the English*

1743
Benjamin Franklin begins his experiments with electricity and founds American Philosophical Society

1751
First volume of French *Encyclopédie* published

1762
Jean-Jacques Rousseau publishes the political treatise *The Social Contract* and the novel *Émile*

1763
Treaty of Paris ends French and Indian War in America

1764
Voltaire publishes the *Philosophical Dictionary*

1765
The 17th and final volume of the French *Encyclopédie* published

1776
American revolution begins with publication of the Declaration of Independence

Adam Smith publishes *The Wealth of Nations*

1786
Caroline Herschel discovers a comet

1787
U.S. Constitution is drafted

1789
French Revolution

Former slave Olaudah Equiano publishes his autobiography

1791
Slave uprising in San Domingue, Haiti

1792
Mary Wollstonecraft publishes *Vindication of the Rights of Woman*

FURTHER READING

Entries with ⟦⟧ indicate primary source material.

GENERAL WORKS ON THE SCIENTIFIC REVOLUTION AND THE ENLIGHTENMENT

Editors of Time-Life Books. *Powers of the Crown: Time Frame AD 1600–1700.* Alexandria, Va.: Time-Life Books, 1989.

Editors of Time-Life Books. *Winds of Revolution: Time Frame AD 1700–1800.* Alexandria, Va.: Time-Life Books, 1990.

ATLASES

Haywood, John. *World Atlas of the Past.* Vol. 3, *The Age of Discovery, 1492 to 1815.* New York: Oxford University Press, 1999.

McEvedy, Colin. *The Penguin Atlas of Modern History (to 1815).* New York: Penguin, 1986.

DICTIONARIES AND ENCYCLOPEDIAS

Applebaum, Wilbur, ed. *Encyclopedia of the Scientific Revolution: From Copernicus to Newton.* New York: Garland, 2000.

Burns, William E. *Science in the Enlightenment: An Encyclopedia.* Santa Barbara, Calif.: ABC-CLIO, 2003.

Delon, Michel, ed. *Encyclopedia of the Enlightenment.* 2 vols. Chicago: Fitzroy Dearborn, 2001.

Edwards, Paul. *The Encyclopedia of Philosophy.* 8 vols. New York: Macmillan, 1967.

Kors, Alan, ed. *Encyclopedia of the Enlightenment.* 4 vols. New York: Oxford University Press, 2003.

Wilson, Ellen Judy. *Encyclopedia of the Enlightenment.* Rev. ed. New York: Facts on File, 2004.

BIOGRAPHY

Gillespie, Charles Coulston, ed. *Dictionary of Scientific Biography.* New York: Scribners, 1981.

Also see individual biographies under subject headings.

CHINA

⟦⟧ Confucius. *Confucian Analects, The Great Learning, and The Doctrine of the Mean.* Translated by James Legge. New York: Dover, 1971.

Dunne, George H. *Generation of Giants. The Story of the Jesuits in China in the Last Decades of the Ming Dynasty.* Notre Dame, Ind.: University of Notre Dame Press, 1962.

Fairbank, John K. *China. A New History.* Cambridge, Mass.: Belknap Press, 1992.

Gardner, Daniel K. *Chu Hsi. Learning to be a Sage.* Berkeley: University of California Press, 1990.

Goodrich, L. Carrington, ed. *Dictionary of Ming Biography.* New York: Columbia University Press, 1976.

Ronan, Charles E., ed. *East Meets West, The Jesuits in China, 1582–1777.* Chicago: Loyola University Press, 1988.

Spence, Jonathan. *The Memory Palace of Matteo Ricci.* New York: Penguin, 1984.

Twitchett, Denis, and Frederick W. Mote, eds. *Cambridge History of China*, vols. 8 and 9. New York: Cambridge University Press, 2002.

DEMOCRACY AND REVOLUTIONS

Bullock, Steven C. *The American Revolution: A History in Documents.* New York: Oxford University Press, 2003.

Dubois, Laurent. *Avengers of the New World: The Story of the Haitian Revolution.* Cambridge, Mass.: Harvard University Press, 2004.

⟦⟧ Franklin, Benjamin. *The Autobiography of Benjamin Franklin & Selections from His Other Writings.* New York: Modern Library, 2001.

Gaustad, Edwin S. *Benjamin Franklin: Inventing America.* New York: Oxford University Press, 2004.

Hunt, Lynn. *The French Revolution and Human Rights: A Brief Documentary History.* Boston: Bedford/St. Martin's, 1996.

Marrin, Albert. *The War for Independence: The Story of the American Revolution.* New York: Atheneum, 1988.

Morgan, Edmund Sears. *Benjamin Franklin*. New Haven, Conn.: Yale University Press, 2002.

66 Schwoerer, Lois G. *The Declaration of Rights, 1689*. Baltimore: Johns Hopkins University Press, 1981

Wood, Gordon. *The American Revolution: A History*. New York: Modern Library, 2002.

THE ENLIGHTENMENT

Andrews, Wayne. *Voltaire*. New York: New Directions, 1981.

Dunn, John M. *The Enlightenment*. San Diego: Lucent, 1999.

Durant, Will, and Ariel Durant. *The Age of Voltaire*, New York: Simon and Schuster, 1965.

Gay, Peter, and the Editors of Time-Life Books. *The Age of Enlightenment*. New York: Time, 1966.

Gillespie, Charles C., ed. *A Diderot Pictorial Encyclopedia of Trades and Industry: 485 Plates Selected from L'Encyclopédie of Dénis Diderot*. New York: Dover, 1993.

Jacob, Margaret C. *The Enlightenment: A Brief History with Documents*. Boston: Bedford/St. Martin's, 2001.

Kramnick, Isaac, ed. *The Portable Enlightenment Reader*. New York: Penguin, 1995.

66 Montesquieu, Baron de. *Persian Letters*. Translated by George R. Healy. Indianapolis: Bobbs-Merrill, 1964.

66 ———. *The Spirit of the Laws*. New York: Cambridge University Press, 1989.

Norton, James R. *Jean-Jacques Rousseau: Advocate of Government by Consent (Leaders of the Enlightenment)*. New York: Rosen Publishing Group, 2005.

Spellman, W. M. *John Locke*. New York: St. Martin's, 1997.

Strathern, Paul. *Locke in 90 Minutes*. Chicago: Ivan R. Dee, 1999.

———. *Rousseau in 90 Minutes*. Chicago: Ivan R. Dee, 2002.

Thomson, Garrett. *On Locke*. Belmont, Calif.: Wadsworth/Thomson Learning, 2001.

ISLAM

Beshore, George. *Science in Early Islamic Culture*. New York: Franklin Watts, 1998.

Esposito, John L., ed. *The Oxford Dictionary of Islam*. New York: Oxford University Press, 2003.

———, ed. *The Oxford History of Islam*. New York: Oxford University Press, 1999.

Glasse, Cyril. *New Encyclopedia of Islam: A Revised Edition of the Concise Encyclopedia of Islam*. Lanham, Md.: Altamira Press, 2003.

Robinson, Francis E., ed. *The Cambridge Illustrated History of the Islamic World*. New York: Cambridge University Press, 1996.

MUGHAL INDIA

Findly, Ellison Banks. *Nur Jahan: Empress of Mughal India*. New York: Oxford University Press, 1993.

66 Jahangir. *The Jahangirnama: Memoirs of Jahangir, Emperor of India*. Translated and edited by Wheeler M. Thackston. New York: Oxford University Press, 1999.

Metcalf, Barbara D., and Thomas R. Metcalf. *A Concise History of India*. New York: Cambridge University Press, 2002.

Richards, John F. *The Mughal Empire*. New York: Cambridge University Press, 1993.

NORTH AMERICAN COLONIES AND TRADE

Allen, Paula Gunn. *Pocahontas: Medicine Woman, Spy, Entrepreneur, Diplomat*. San Francisco: HarperSanFrancisco, 2003.

Brown, Gene. *Discovery and Settlement: Europe Meets the New World, 1490–1700*. New York: Twenty-First Century Books, 1993.

Campbell, R. H. *Adam Smith*. New York: St. Martin's, 1982.

Doherty, Kieran. *Puritans, Pilgrims, and Merchants: Founders of the Northeastern Colonies*. Minneapolis: Oliver Press, 1999.

———. *To Conquer Is to Live: The Life of Captain John Smith of Jamestown*. Brookfield, Conn.: Twenty-First Century Books, 2001.

Fritz, Jean. *The Double Life of Pocahontas*. New York: Putnam, 1983.

Gray, Edward G. *Colonial America: A History in Documents*. New York: Oxford University Press, 2003.

Howard, Thomas, ed. *Black Voyage: Eyewitness Accounts of the Atlantic Slave Trade*. Boston: Little, Brown, 1971.

Hume, Ivor Noel. *The Virginia Adventure: Roanoke to James Towne: An Archaeological and Historical Odyssey*. New York: Knopf, 1994.

Jaycox, Faith. *The Colonial Era: An Eyewitness History*. New York: Facts on File, 2002.

Kupperman, Karen Ordahl. *Indians and English.* Ithaca, N.Y.: Cornell University Press, 2000.

Lepore, Jill. *Early American Encounters: A History in Documents.* New York: Oxford University Press, 2000.

Middleton, Richard. *Colonial America: A History, 1585–1776.* New York: Oxford University Press, 2000.

Price, David. *Love and Hate in Jamestown: John Smith, Pocahontas, and the Heart of a New Nation.* New York: Knopf, 2003.

66 Smith, Adam. *The Essential Adam Smith.* Edited by Robert L. Heilbroner. New York: Norton, 1986.

66 ———. *Inquiry into the Nature and Causes of the Wealth of Nations.* Edited by Edwin Cannan. New York: Modern Library, 2000.

Taylor, Alan. *American Colonies: The Settling of North America.* New York: Penguin, 2001.

Weber, Max. *The Protestant Ethic and the Spirit of Capitalism.* New York: Scribners, 1958.

Wood, Peter H. *Strange New Land: African Americans, 1617–1776.* New York: Oxford University Press, 1996.

THE OTTOMAN EMPIRE

Blair, Sheila, and Jonathan Bloom. *The Art and Architecture of Islam, 1250–1800.* New Haven, Conn.: Yale University Press, 1994.

Imber, Colin. *The Ottoman Empire, 1300–1650: The Structure of Power.* New York: Palgrave Macmillan, 2002.

Kinross, Patrick. *The Ottoman Centuries: The Rise and Fall of the Turkish Empire.* New York: Morrow, 1977.

Macauley, David. *Mosque.* Boston: Houghton Mifflin, 2003.

Montagu, Lady Mary Wortley. *Selected Letters.* Edited by Isobel Grundy. New York: Penguin, 1997.

THE SCIENTIFIC REVOLUTION

Christianson, Gale E. *Isaac Newton and the Scientific Revolution.* New York: Oxford University Press, 1996.

Conant, James Bryant. *The Overthrow of the Phlogiston Theory: The Chemical Revolution of 1775–1789.* Cambridge, Mass.: Harvard University Press, 1966

66 Copernicus, Nicolaus. *On the Revolutions of the Heavenly Spheres.* A. M. Duncan, trans. New York: Barnes & Noble, 1976.

Drake, Stillman, ed. and trans. *Discoveries and Opinions of Galileo,* New York: Doubleday, 1957.

Finocchiaro, Maurice A. *The Galileo Affair: A Documentary History.* Berkeley: University of California Press, 1989.

Gingerich, Owen, and James MacLachlan. *Nicolaus Copernicus: Making the Earth a Planet.* New York: Oxford University Press, 2005.

Henry, John. *The Scientific Revolution and the Origins of Modern Science,* 2nd ed. New York: Palgrave Macmillan, 2002.

Huff, Toby E. *The Rise of Early Modern Science: Islam, China, and the West.* 2nd ed. New York: Cambridge University Press, 2003.

Jardine, Lisa. *Ingenious Pursuits: Building the Scientific Revolution.* New York: Doubleday, 1999.

MacLachlan, James. *Galileo Galilei: First Physicist.* New York: Oxford University Press, 1997.

Margolis, Harold. *It Started with Copernicus: How Turning the World Inside Out Led to the Scientific Revolution.* New York: McGraw-Hill, 2002.

Shackelford, Jole. *William Harvey and the Mechanics of the Heart.* New York: Oxford University Press, 2003.

Voelkel, James R. *Johannes Kepler and the New Astronomy.* New York: Oxford University Press, 1999.

WOMEN AND THE SALONS

Brody, Miriam. *Mary Wollstonecraft: Mother of Women's Rights.* New York: Oxford University Press, 2000.

Grundy, Isobel. *Lady Mary Wortley Montagu.* New York: Oxford University Press, 1999.

Hill, Bridget. *Eighteenth-Century Women.* London: Allen & Unwin, 1987.

Landes, Joan. *Women and the Public Sphere in the Age of the French Revolution.* Ithaca, N.Y.: Cornell University Press, 1988.

66 Montagu, Lady Mary. *The Complete Letters of Lady Wortley Montagu,* ed. by R. Halsband. Oxford: Clarendon Press, 1965.

66 ———. *Turkish Embassy Letters.* Edited by Malcolm Jack. Athens: University of Georgia Press, 1993.

Stott, Anne. *Hannah More: The First Victorian.* New York: Oxford University Press, 2003.

66 Wollestoncraft, Mary. *A Vindication of the Rights of Woman: With Strictures on Political and Moral Subjects.* Edited by Miriam Brody. New York: Penguin, 1993.

WEBSITES

Africans in America: The Terrible Transformation 1450–1750
www.pbs.org/wgbh/aia/part1/title.html
Sponsored by PBS, this site provides a detailed look at the slave trade and the middle passage.

Conquistadors
www.pbs.org/opb/conquistadors/home.htm
This PBS-sponsored site explores the history of the Spanish in the New World, focusing on their impact on Native Americans.

The Encyclopedia of Diderot & d'Alembert
www.hti.umich.edu/d/did/
Sponsored by the University of Michigan, this site features translations of articles from the *Encyclopédie*. Click on the "Browse" link to select article topics.

The Galileo Project
http://galileo.rice.edu/
Sponsored by Rice University, this site describes itself as "a source of information on the life and work of Galileo Galilei."

History of the Microscope
www.cas.muohio.edu/~mbi-ws/microscopes/ history.html
A site sponsored by Miami University in Ohio that explores microscopes and their invention.

The Internet Encyclopedia of Philosophy
www.utm.edu/research/iep
The University of Tennessee at Martin hosts this online encyclopedia, which includes biographies of philosophers such as John Locke and Hugo Grotius.

The Legacy of Islamic Empires and Their Arts
www.islamicart.com/library/empires/india/
This site explores the architectural achievements of the Mughal Empire in India. Click on the "shahjahan" link for information about the Taj Mahal.

The Ottomans
www.theottomans.org/english/index.asp
An informative site on all aspects of the Ottoman Empire, including art and culture.

Virtual Jamestown
http://www.virtualjamestown.org/
A collaboration between Virginia Tech, the University of Virginia, and the Virginia Center for Digital History at the University of Virginia, this expanding site features a number of primary sources, including letters and court records, from the early days of the Jamestown colony.

VOC Shipwrecks: Geldermalsen
www.vocshipwrecks.nl/home_voyages3/ geldermalsen.html
The in-depth story of the 1752 shipwreck of the Geldermalsen.

The Wealth of Nations
http://www.bartleby.com/10/
The text from the abridged Harvard Classics edition of Adam Smith's *The Wealth of Nations*.

Welcome to the Salons of Paris
www.mtholyoke.edu/courses/rschwart/hist255-s01/ paris_homework/welcome_to_salons.html
A look at the salons of Paris with an emphasis on women's influence, sponsored by Mount Holyoke College.

INDEX

References to illustrations and their captions are indicated by page numbers in **bold**.

TEXT AND PICTURE CREDITS

TEXT CREDITS

P. 20: Kupperman, Karen Ordahl, *Indians & English* (Ithaca, N.Y.: Cornell University Press, 2000), 46.

P. 21: Hudson, J. Paul, *A Pictorial Story of Jamestown, Virginia: The Voyage and Search for a Settlement Site* (Richmond, Va.: Garrett and Massie, 1957), 44.

P. 23: Kupperman, *Indians & English*, 92.

P. 32–33: Falconbridge, Alexander, *An account of the slave trade on the coast of Africa* (London: James Phillips, 1788), 29–47.

P. 37: Kramnick, Isaac, ed. *The Portable Enlightenment Reader* (New York: Penguin, 1995), 506.

P. 41: Weber, Max, *The Protestant Ethic and the Spirit of Capitalism* (New York: Scribner's, 1958), 175.

P. 42: Kramnick, *The Portable Enlightenment Reader*, 508.

P. 44: Kramnick, *The Portable Enlightenment Reader*, 507.

P. 49: Miller, Barnette, *The Palace School of Muhammad the Conqueror* (Cambridge, Mass.: Harvard University Press, 1941), 5.

P. 56: Hattox, Ralph S. P., *Coffee and the Coffeehouses: The Origins of a Social Beverage in the Medieval Near East* (Seattle: University of Washington Press, 1985), 81.

P. 57: Montagu, Mary Wortley, Lady, *Letters of the Right Honourable Lady M—y W—y M—e: Written, during her Travels in Europe, Asia and Africa, to Persons of Distinction, Men of Letters. &c., in different Parts of Europe* (Dublin: Printed for P. Wilson, J. Hoey, Junior, and J. Potts, Booksellers, 1763), 138–39.

P. 63: Thackston, Wheeler, ed., *The Jahangirnama: Memoirs of Jahangir, Emperor of India* (New York: Oxford University Press, 1999), xix.

P. 65: Andrea, Alfred J., and James H. Overfield, *The Human Record: Sources of Global History*, 5th ed., vol. 2 (Boston: Houghton Mifflin, 2005), 54.

P. 67: TK

P. 74: Spence, Jonathan, *To Change China: Western Advisers in China, 1620–1960* (Boston: Little, Brown, 1969), 6–7.

P. 76: Spence, *To Change China: Western Advisers in China, 1620–1960*, 22–23.

P. 78–79: Gardner, Daniel K., ed., *Learning to Be a Sage: Selections from the Conversations of Master Chu, Arranged Topically* (Berkeley: University of California Press, 1990), 29–30.

P. 83: Spence, *To Change China: Western Advisers in China, 1620–1960*, 28.

P. 85: Spence, *To Change China: Western Advisers in China, 1620–1960*, 18–19.

P. 89: Boorstin, Daniel J., *The Discoverers: A History of Man's Search to Know His World and Himself* (New York: Random House, 1983), 300–301.

P. 92: Hazard, Paul, *The European Mind 1680–1715* (Cleveland: World Publishing, 1963), 304–305.

P. 95: MacLachlan, James, *Galileo Galilei: First Scientist* (New York: Oxford University Press, 1997), 76.

P. 98: Boorstin, *The Discoverers: A History of Man's Search to Know His World and Himself*, 310.

P. 99: Boorstin, *The Discoverers: A History of Man's Search to Know His World and Himself*, 309.

P. 100: Boorstin, *The Discoverers: A History of Man's Search to Know His World and Himself*, 319.

P. 104: Boorstin, *The Discoverers: A History of Man's Search to Know His World and Himself*, 367.

P. 107: Conant, James Bryant, *The Overthrow of the Phlogiston Theory: The Chemical Revolution of 1775–1789* (Cambridge, Mass.: Harvard University Press, 1966), 43–44.

P. 113: Christianson, Gale E., *Isaac Newton and the Scientific Revolution* (New York: Oxford University Press, 1996), 84.

P. 114: Christianson, *Isaac Newton and the Scientific Revolution*, 68–69.

P. 118: Kramnick, *The Portable Enlightenment Reader*, 115–116.

P. 119: Kramnick, *The Portable Enlightenment Reader*, 116.

P. 121: Montesquieu, Charles de Secondat, Baron de, *The Spirit of the Laws*. Reprint, ed. trans. Anne M. Cohler, Basia Carolyn Miller, Harold Samuel Stone (Cambridge: Cambridge University Press, 1989), 10–11.

P. 122: Hyland, Paul, ed., *The Enlightenment: A Sourcebook and Reader* (New York: Routledge, 2003), 168.

P. 131: Goodman, Dena, *The Republic of Letters: A Cultural History of the French Enlightenment* (Ithaca, N.Y.: Cornell University Press, 1994), 114.

P. 133: Brody, Miriam, *Mary Wollstonecraft: Mother of Women's Rights* (New York: Oxford University Press, 2000), 82.

P. 136: Goodman, *The Republic of Letters: A Cultural History of the French Enlightenment*, 101.

P. 138: Hill, Bridget, *Eighteenth Century Women* (London: Allen & Unwin, 1984), 55–56.

P. 140: Todd, Janet, ed., *The Collected Letters of Mary Wollstonecraft* (London: Allen Lane, 2003), 139.

P. 142: Hyland, *The Enlightenment: A Sourcebook and Reader,* 155.

P. 145: Hyland, *The Enlightenment: A Sourcebook and Reader,* 154.

P. 148: Hyland, *The Enlightenment: A Sourcebook and Reader,* 154.

P. 150–51: Schwoerer, Lois G., *The Declaration of Rights, 1689* (Baltimore: Johns Hopkins University Press, 1981), 296–97.

P. 153: Franklin, Benjamin, *The Autobiography of Benjamin Franklin & Selections from His Writings* (New York: Illustrated Modern Library, 1944), 208.

P. 157: Clark, Ronald W., *Benjamin Franklin: A Biography* (New York: Random House, 1983), 312.

P. 160: Kramnick, *The Portable Enlightenment Reader,* 551.

TOBY E. HUFF is a sociologist who has studied comparative historical development in the civilizations of Islam, China, and the West. A senior research associate in the Center for Policy Analysis at the University of Massachusetts at Dartmouth, he is the author of *The Rise of Early Modern Science: Islam, China, and the West*. Professor Huff has been a visiting scholar at the University of Malaya, the National University of Singapore, and in the Center for Middle Eastern Studies at Harvard University. During the summer of 2001 he lived for four months in Kuala Lumpur, Malaysia, studying Malaysia's Multimedia Super Corridor, the most advanced Internet project in the Muslim world. He has traveled and lectured widely in Europe, the Middle East, and southeastern Asia.

BONNIE G. SMITH is Board of Governors Professor of History at Rutgers University. She has edited a series for teachers on Women's and Gender History in Global Perspective for the American Historical Association and has served as chair of the test development committee for the Advanced Placement examination in European history. Professor Smith is the author of many books on European, comparative, and women's history, among them *Confessions of a Concierge* and *Imperialism: A History in Documents*. She is co-author of *The Making of the West: Peoples and Cultures*, editor in chief of the forthcoming Oxford encyclopedia on women in world history, and general editor of an Oxford world history series for high school students and general readers.

9/25